A Community Remembers

HISTON ROAD

Alison Wilson

with Anna Crutchley and Lilian Rundblad

Photography, Faruk Kara

HRARA

First published in Great Britain by Histon Road Area Residents Association (HRARA) in 2021

ISBN 978-1-5272-9543-8

Printed and bound in Wales by Cambrian Printers,
The Pensord Group, Tram Road, Pontllanfraith NP12 2YA
Designed by Paul Allitt (www.paulallitt.com)
Copy edited and proofread by Ros Horton (r.horton@camedit.com)

Faruk Kara: www.faruk.kara.org.uk
HRARA email: histonroadara@gmail.com
HRARA website: www.facebook.com/histonroadra
and www.histonroadmemories.uk

CONTENTS

Mary Benson
279.1.8
Freehold
Marie Benson 6.2.11
Marie Benson 6.1.10
Marie Benson 6.1.24
10th Allotment The Devisee of Mary Benson 24.1.15 Freehold
Second Allotment to Robert Sparrow the elder 14.2.35 Freehold
William Wragg 10.3.39 Co. Rect
1st Allotment to William Wragg 51:1:16 Co. Ches
William Wragg 13.1.25 Freehold
Prior Sparrow
Thomas Hall Fisher Leasehold
Thomas Hall Fisher 3.1.16 Co Ches
Thomas Hall Fisher 3.2.0 Freehold
Thomas Riddel 2.2.19 Freehold
Thomas Riddel 6.0.16 Co. Ch.
William Wragg. 35.3.20 Co. Merton
Catharine Hall
56.3.7 Freehold
1st Allotment to William Wragg 12.0.0 Freehold
2nd Allotment to William Wragg 6.2.33 Co. Ches
The Second Allotment to Mary Wragg 174.3.0 Freehold
Wragg Freehold
36.0.9
Mary Wragg 66.1.05 Co. Chest
John Haviland 11.3.36 Co. Ches
1st Allot to John Haviland 19.2.38 Freehold
Richard Holt Smales 16.2.25 Freehold
Mary Wragg 3.2.0 Co. Rect
Robert Moore
William Custance 15.3.21 Freehold
Myles Custance 12.0.16
Myles Custance 15.2.29 Co. Chest
Ann Beales 15.2.38 Leasehold 2000 years
First Allot to The Master Fellows and Scholars of Clare Hall 22.2.34 Freehold
Ann Beales 8.3.28 Freehold
Henry Headley the elder
3rd Allotment to the Devisee of Mary Benson Freehold
County Gaol
D L E F I E L D
E S T F I E L D
HUNTINGDON Turnpike ROAD
GILES'S PARISH CAMBRIDGE.

Introduction

Historical background

Histon Road began as an ancient track that may well date back to the Iron Age. It travels in a straight line from the top of Castle Hill to Arbury Camp, a late Iron Age fort (c.200 BC), which lies alongside the present road from Cambridge to Impington and Histon. Iron Age finds have been made in both villages, and possible round burial barrows have been identified. In 2008, archaeological excavations on land belonging to the National Institute of Agricultural Botany (NIAB), between Histon Road and Huntingdon Road, identified two distinct areas of mid to late Iron Age occupation, together with evidence for an inter-joining field system. There were also post holes indicating a late Bronze Age structure. Even earlier are some very fine stone axes from the Neolithic period found in Histon, one of them made of polished jadeite from the Alps.

The Romans were very active in Cambridge, the crossing point of two of their major roads, Akeman Street and Via Devana, (present day Huntingdon Road). They bridged the river and built a fortress on the hill, close to the southern end of what is now Histon Road. It seems certain that they would have had a route across to Histon, which is thought to have been quite a prosperous Roman village with at least one villa and two farms. Roman Akeman Street followed the line of what was later Stretten Avenue and Carlton Way (not the recent street of the same name that is at right-angles to Histon Road) and skirted Impington before bending north-east to Ely.

Histon and Impington are both Saxon names. There has even been speculation that Histon, possibly meaning 'warrior's town', was the home of a Saxon prince. After the Romans left, the Saxons continued farming the fertile land around Histon, and ridge and furrow marks can still be detected there. In the eighth century, King Offa is thought to have created a 'burh' or fortified urban centre on the promontory above the river, guarding the bridge lower down. This was more extensive than the castle mound, forming a large rectangle around it with Histon Road junction at the top and the line of present-day Northampton Street at the bottom. It was not just a garrison;

Copy of the 1840 Enclosure map for the Parish of Chesterton.

more like a small market town to which people from surrounding villages would have brought their produce along roads and tracks such as the one to Histon.

Both Histon and Impington appear in the Domesday Book, a register of land and property taken after the Norman Conquest, and in 1068 the Normans built their own castle, demolishing 27 houses on the site of the burh. Our road was called Histon Way by 1300, and by then Histon was one of the largest villages in Cambridgeshire. The road ran through three open fields, mainly arable and probably cultivated on a triennial rotation from the Middle Ages until their enclosure in 1838. Enclosure maps of the 1850s show Histon Road as a well-established route, 40 feet wide. The three great fields are marked as East, Middle and West. After enclosure, these were divided into parcels of land, large and small, owned by private citizens, the Colleges and charities.

Local resident Clive Bowring has researched this period.

I found out as much as I can about the land, which was probably in strip – it was being strip farmed from medieval times and probably in the 15th or 16th century right through until 1840 when this particular part of Cambridge and its outer fields [was divided up] … And by Act of Parliament, the Enclosure Act apportioned these strips to different owners and some of them very large in size of many, many, many acres. And some of them, those … getting closer to Huntington Road, the south end and Victoria Road were quite small parcels of land sold to people who were interested in developing houses. A lot of them are terraced houses, of course, dating from the middle of the 19th century.

Mary Benson was one of the large landowners, holding many plots north of the river, and Benson Street, which joins Huntingdon Road to Histon Road via Canterbury Street, is named after her. It was most unusual for a single woman to have such large and valuable holdings. William Custance, a businessman who mapped central Cambridge in 1798, bought a plot on the corner of Huntingdon Road and Histon Road as a strategic site for house building. The 19th century was to see rapid expansion of Chesterton north of the river between what were now turnpike roads (Huntingdon and Milton Roads) with many narrow criss-crossing streets forming 'New Chesterton'. The *Cambridge Chronicle* for this period has advertisements for plots of freehold building ground, terraced houses such as 8, 9 and 10 Histon Road

(1876), and even a tenement and brewhouse on the corner of Bermuda Road (1849), all to be sold by auction.

In the following chapters we will attempt to follow the whole length of Histon Road from the south end to the city border. It is worth noting that before the building of the A14 junction, the road to Histon was straighter than it is now at the north end, going west from just before King's Hedges Road, past the farm (Ash Cottage), which is still there, to Cambridge Road and Station Road in Histon before rejoining the B1049 at Water Lane.

The residents of Histon Road find themselves living in a time of further change for the area. Their road, which not so long ago was relatively minor, has, because of the A14 junction, become a major route into Cambridge. As the Cambridge workforce has been pushed by rising house prices out into the villages, traffic has increased year by year. We realised in 2019 that plans to widen the road and put in a bus lane and wider cycle lanes, as well as reducing vegetation, were going to remove the last vestiges of the countryside and turn it into an arterial route. Consequently, it was a moment to capture people's memories of the past before they were overlaid by stressful events. What we could not have known was that 2020 would be the year when everything changed nationally because of the coronavirus. Our final public meeting, celebrating the success of the project, was held only days before the government lockdown. Fortunately we had collected the testimonies of nearly 30 people, some going back as far as World War II.

'A Community Remembers: Histon Road' was the brainchild of Lilian Rundblad, a Swedish national who had been living close to Histon Road for 12 years. She had become interested in the history of the area, collecting information from people she met, so when Cambridge City Council announced an Area Committee Community Grant she had a ready-made project to propose. Several neighbours answered the call to join in: two of them, an archivist and a librarian, had carried out oral history interviewing before; another was running a local group, and one was a semi-professional photographer. This was enough to get the scope of the grant proposal worked out; other helpers were recruited later.

The eight public meetings were deliberately held on both sides of the road, utilising community venues such as The Meadows and Bermuda Community Room (Arbury ward) and the Lutheran Church Hall and Mayfield School (Castle ward). Local historian and creator of the Cambridgeshire Collection, Mike Petty, spoke at the first three, and was immensely helpful in providing material throughout.

Histon Road view looking south, 1963. Below: The same view in 2020.

Oral communication was key to this project, with the informal nature of the meetings encouraging people to voice their memories and interact with each other. Some of them offered to give short talks or written accounts of topics ranging from allotments to the cemetery and pre-war Roseford Road. There were plenty of volunteers for one-to-one interviews, which were carried out in residents' homes. This book attempts to sort their memories into a continuous narrative, including as many as possible. All the recordings and their transcripts will be available for posterity in the Museum of Cambridge. We should make clear that this book is not intended to give a complete history of Histon Road, since the content is dependent on the information presented by those who chose to take part.

Mike Petty.

The second aspect of the project was the photographic record of the participants and the Histon Road environment. Historic photographs encouraged 'then and now' comparisons of buildings and street scenes. Our photographer, Faruk Kara, also showed a remarkable talent for capturing unusual or arresting aspects of people and places; he steadily built up a portfolio that documents Histon Road at this particular point in time. Two exhibitions of his work are planned.

Faruk writes:

My challenge has been to present familiar subjects and locations, which are often dry in content, such that the audience discovers and looks at them differently. It is also to create a documentary record for future generations in an interesting and engaging way.

Examining a map and photographs at a meeting.

Histon Road Co-op manager, Antony Finn.

The organising team were constantly surprised by what they discovered. Quite a few well-known people have lived or worked in this relatively small area, including P. D. James, Clive Sinclair, David Parr (decorative artist), Charles Alverson (screenplay for the film *Jabberwocky*), Alison Hennegan (campaigner for LGBT rights) and former Mayor Gerri Bird. The poor housing conditions in the 1930s are vividly remembered by some of our older contributors, as are the wartime circumstances – sirens, air raids, demolishing of railings for salvage, rationing and the prisoners of war working in the fields. We discovered a network of people who had spent their whole lives in this area, or had gone away and returned here later. In addition, there were close-knit groups connected with housing, such as the Bermuda flats and the Bangladeshi community in Histon Road and Darwin Drive or social groups such as the Cemetery Committee, Mayfield Seniors and the Residents' Associations. It was a very rewarding exercise. About half-way through the project, Anna Crutchley recorded the impressions of one of the committee.

And I really have enjoyed it. I'm still enjoying it, more, I think as I see the benefits for the community, because as well as collecting information our aim was to involve people in their surroundings and help them to meet and get to know each other, sort of strengthen their ties with the area and with each other. And that just works so well. When you remember, we've had four meetings so far and at each one we've had some kind of surprise really, somebody popping up; it's wonderful information. And other people contributing and saying, 'oh, yes, I remember that'. And then they just sit and chat and it's all very convivial …

Anna Crutchley highlighted a lovely moment when two members in their eighties recognised each other at one of the meetings: as children, they had lived in adjacent streets. We also had people who seldom meet exchanging memories about Roseford Road and the big VE Day party held in a field at the end, and there were residents interested in the cemetery because their relatives were buried there.

Histon Road is the sort of area one could easily overlook. For some people it is just a conduit to the A14. Unless you live there you might never explore the side roads. Alison Wilson had lived in various different parts of Cambridge for over 40 years before moving to the McManus Estate in 2014.

Audience at the final meeting. Front row: Ann Whitmore, David Lawrence, Anna Crutchley.

It was really a new area to me. I hadn't a clue what it would be like. And actually, different parts of Cambridge are very different and in quite small areas there's a sort of identity.

This is what we were looking to discover. Histon Road has no real coherence in its planning and few outstanding buildings, but as Anna remarked:

There's a lot going on in terms of shops and residents and so on. Underneath it all there is this community, isn't there … And it's absolutely fascinating.

The Grapes and the Tandoori Palace, formerly the Prince of Wales pub.

The city end of Histon Road

Local residents and businesses

Ronald Pryor (1922–2011) lived at 10 Histon Road and wrote down his childhood memories to hand down to his family. His marvellous drawing (overleaf) shows the Huntingdon, Histon and Victoria Road junction in 1930, with the Victoria Tavern at the apex, Rudd's garage, Bilton's bakehouse, and a terrace of houses starting with his home at number 10. The road was quiet, with the milkman on his horse and cart working his way towards the junction. A barrow boy and muffin man ringing his bell are walking towards him.

On the other side of Histon Road, the corner site had originally been a women's seminary, called Chestnut House, run by a Mrs Lawson. Later on, Ann Whitmore remembers when there was a car showroom at the opposite corner where Nido, a student accommodation block, now stands.

The top of Histon Road I well remember … it was a garage … and it took the whole of that corner. There was the great big glass showrooms and then there were the chains around the side and we had to swing on those chains. You know, that would just be a lovely thing to play with.

David Keyworth remembers it as Murketts' Corner, and some people still call the site by that name, which must be confusing for those who have come to live in the area since Murketts' moved further down to 137 Histon Road. This corner site was opened in 1931, when Murketts' already had premises in Huntingdon, Bedford and Peterborough. Dennis Murkett was a 'whitesmith' living in Huntingdon who dealt in and repaired bicycles when they were still a novelty. He died in 1891 and his eldest son, Harry, and Harry's younger brothers succeeded him, founding Murkett Bros. in 1893. They went on to work on motor tricycles and after World War II when the motor car started to become popular, they began to deal in second-hand cars and take on car repairs. According to legend, the Murketts were never in bed after 4.30 am and remained in the workshop until 10 pm. Also, according to legend, the first motorcycle sent to Norway was manufactured by Murketts'.

The building became a petrol filling station run by Texaco and then for a number of years when it was waiting to be demolished, became a hand

Ronald Pryor's view of the Histon Road junction in 1930.

HISTON ROAD
VICTORIA
HUNTINGDON ROAD
HUNTINGDON RD HISTON RD VICTORIA RD 1930 RH PRYOR

Murkett Bros., 1931.

car wash run by very efficient east Europeans. But David bemoans the loss of the showroom.

Well, they had a lovely Art Deco showroom. I mean today they would never have been able to demolish it. Huge plate glass windows.

The garage had gained some further space when the newsagent between it and the Grapes pub on Histon Road burnt down.

So, it becomes a little confusing, and indeed placing past local businesses according to residents' memories is not always an exact science.

In 1997, some time after the site had become a petrol station, Texaco put in a planning application to open a Burger King. Drivers travelling south on Histon and Victoria Roads used to cross the Histon Road north-bound lane to enter the petrol station grounds. In itself this was a tricky manoeuvre, but if you can imagine drivers queuing to enter a Burger King site, blocking the left-hand lane on Huntingdon Road and the north-bound lane on Histon Road, then this becomes even more dangerous. That, and the possibility of drivers leaving the site to make way for more customers, clenching a burger between their teeth as they started to move off, was anathema to local residents who objected to the application. John Sutcliffe drew a Burger King look-alike poster with 'Burger Off' written on it to advertise residents' objections, but this was quietly abandoned as it was mooted that Burger King would surely sue. Luckily, the application was refused.

The recently built student accommodation there was named Chestnut House in commemoration of its origins, before it was sold after a year or so and renamed Nido, the Italian word for a nest, which sounds more inviting.

What is now Cranwell Court, a block of flats next to Nido, was a vegetable garden belonging to 9 Huntingdon Road. No. 9 had been built much later than its neighbours, hence being the only house with an odd number on that side of the road. It had large gardens with a handsome coach house and orchard backing onto North Street, and the vegetable garden and a pair of garages onto Histon Road.

Near the top of Histon Road next to Cranwell Court is the Grapes pub, the last remaining pub on Histon Road after the Victoria Tavern was knocked down, the Prince of Wales was transformed into Tandoori Palace, an Indian restaurant and take-away, and the British Queen was demolished and the site redeveloped as the Lucy Cavendish college hostel. The Grapes earns its reputation as a proper 'local', and its regulars include many residents of the Histon Road area. John and Gabrielle Sutcliffe used to live at 12 Huntingdon Road and their back gate opened out directly opposite the entrance to the Grapes back yard on North Street. They have been regulars there for over 35 years, and when they eventually decided to downsize, they moved to a smaller terraced house on Histon Road, and recruited their builders from the crowd they knew at the Grapes. Their house, 151 Histon Road, and its three neighbouring properties had been hit by a Wellington bomber returning home from a bombing raid in Germany in 1941, and when renovating their house, they discovered the effects of that crash. John tells us:

Barry was six feet underground doing the drains, which I think got damaged by the aeroplane because the soil stack, which is cast iron, goes into pot drains, and I think when it was bashed at the top, it broke the pot drains underneath, so they were pretty much shot …

John also tells us:

The picture on the ceiling is a poster from an exhibition at the Royal Academy from back in the '80s I suppose, as printed for the display on the underground, which is why it's so big … And, so it was in our house in Norfolk, it was in 153a, it was in Huntingdon Road and now it's on the ceiling here at 151 – the only Veronese on a ceiling on Histon Road – probably!

John Sutcliffe in his library.

Norma Davies lives in Windsor Road and rarely walked up to the south end of Histon Road but remembers buying shoes there for her daughter, Alison.

There was a little haberdasher. I think it was called Norman's up that end. And I bought your first shoes from that little shop up there.

Rosemarie Hutchinson lived at 67 Histon Road as a child and remembers:

There was a butcher on Histon Road. He was called Mr Welch and his, uh, assistant was called Frank Harvey. And he lived next door to us and he'd bring us home rabbits and skin them up …

Mr Welch.

In 2015, Syrian entrepreneur Marwa Kuwaider took over what was Nasreen Dar at 18–20 Histon Road. She renamed it Midan, an Arabic word for a town square and meeting place. In Damascus, where she comes from, the midan was open day and night for groceries and exotic foods. During the height of the first coronavirus lockdown in spring 2020, with its severe food shortages, it was one of the few places you could buy flour, yeast and rice.

Previously it had been a grocery store owned by Mahmood Mohammed Darr who originally emigrated to Cambridge to work as a foreman at Playfair Works, a sports factory run by the Gray family on Benson Street. The company had started elsewhere in 1855, and when the factory was eventually demolished in 1986, Mahmood and his wife set up Nasreen Dar, which became a delightful, and essential, convenience store. Forever changing and innovating, they took over the house next door so it became a double width shop, and more recently Mahmood's son Kashif ran a coffee bar for people to sit and enjoy some sociable time together. Before that it was Malcolm's Meats, and before that again, Welch's the butchers.

Meanwhile, back near the top of the street, David Keyworth noted Arbury Fast-Fit at 33–35 Histon Road, which fixes car tyres and exhausts, and used to be Ison's Granary.

Oh, yes. That was Ison's. Bill Ison was a real character. He was an ex-wartime pilot. He had a little Tiger Moth at Marshall's. Yellow Tiger Moth biplane. And he used to fly around at the weekends. Well, that was his, and we call it a granary, I don't know, but it was an agricultural feed merchants, I think you might say … you could go there and get your chicken feed, your poultry feed, the poultry and chickens … pig feed I was thinking. And probably get budgie seed as well, I don't know. And that packed up and we then had Betabake, who were a big bread distribution company. They baked bread in Ipswich, and that came in a big articulated lorry. They had little electric delivery vans. And they were loaded up and they went all over the place.

Arbury Fast-fit, formerly Ison's.

Ison's Granary at 143 Histon Road.

Jo-Anne Kocian jovially remembers walking past Arbury Fast-Fit one day:

I was walking home from work and saw some men in blue overalls dancing – and I thought what are they doing? And as I passed, I could see some cameras filming them; and I later saw why – they were filming part of the Kwik Fit advertisement. I saw it on television.

How many of us remember these boys in blue dancing together to the Kwik Fit ditty in 1984, 'You can't get better than a Kwik Fit fitter'?

Michael French has found out more about Herbert Ison who founded the business and is buried in the Histon Road Cemetery. Frederick Herbert Ison (1894 –1964) lived at 140 Histon Road. In 1925–26 he acquired the site opposite his home on Histon Road, now ATS Euromaster at no. 143, and built a granary to store the grain and products he was buying and selling. His sons, who included Bill, continued in the business, which closed down in 1968. The Arbury Fast-Fit building was their second site.

A well-known business that had its beginnings as part of the Cambridge technology boom in the 1960s was Cambridge Consultants, which gradually moved into 69 Histon Road, now the home of Headlines Hairdressers. It belonged to Rodney Dale who had set up Polyhedron Solutions, a printing business. Within a year Polyhedron had morphed into an electronics consultancy and prototype developer called Cambridge Consultants. It is now a multi-million-pound organisation with offices in the Milton Road Science Park, the USA, Japan and Singapore, but you would never have guessed that by the stories Rodney tells of its origins. In *From Ram Yard to Milton Hilton* he relates stories of the early development of the site with mirth, the company reeling from one calamity to another.

Inside 69 were several fascinating features – nooks and crannies, trap-doors, Siamese cat-scratching posts, the history of wallpaper – layer upon layer starting with William Morris – attached at skirting board level and swaying drunkenly towards the middle of the room at the top, the plaster fruit round the ceiling of the main room upstairs, the rising damp, original mahogany counter, and the 'secret cellar' (more like a small sump) in which, it was rumoured, the late Mr Westrop [the previous owner] had hidden his unbanked millions.

According to a map of 1860, the back yard of 69 Histon Road had always been packed with outbuildings to left and right, with a garden path down the middle. The buildings included a bakery, and although some had been pulled down over the years, Rodney added to the workshops, roofing over more of the premises to make room for instrument makers.

There was a clear strip of garden stretching down to North Street, ripe for the next phase of expansion. So, they commissioned a large custom-built asbestos shed, but unfortunately someone took the measurements from the wrong side of the tape. When the monster building was delivered, they had some problems in reconciling reality to expectation. This building had no planning permission, of course, but we believed that if it were a temporary building none was needed. Accordingly, we printed some large notices saying TEMPORARY BUILDING and stuck them all over it.

Rodney used his printing business to produce leaflets explaining the delay in delivery of Clive Sinclair's latest invention. They had started selling it in advance in order to finance the purchase of new parts but it had proved so successful that they couldn't keep up with demand. As the more technologically clever items started to be designed and prototyped, Rodney revealed:

It soon became apparent that to make successful things something additional to enthusiasm was needed (we call it 'skill') and an advertisement was put in the Cambridge paper for instrument makers.

In 1981, they eventually took over the building he calls the Milton Hilton on the new Milton Road Science Park – a proud step up from their modest first sites, which included no. 69 and a bedsit in Ram Yard, just off Bridge Street, where the multi-storey car park is now.

Rosemarie Hutchinson lived next door, and Clive Sinclair would pass her a coin to guard his car when he visited no. 69. She also remembers a well on the ground floor of no. 67, much like Rodney Dale's sump. Her family used to throw rubbish into the well to fill it.

In a series of articles on Histon Road in the *Cambridge Weekly News* in 1990, Dan Jackson writes that 'Histon Road has never been a road for the rich', and Ann Whitmore remembers the poverty of her childhood at 75a. An indication of the recession of the '30s was the soup club run by St John's College. Ann remembers 'they were hard times'. She used to go to the College kitchens with a large container and wait while a little ceremony was performed.

It would all be laid out with a little table and there'd be a tray and there'd be a silver dish and a silver spoon. This is what it looked like to us … I used to think it was the Master of the College, and it possibly could have been. But whoever it was, they were in gown and mortar board, and they would come up to go up the steps and they would take one taste of the soup. And if they thought it was good enough, they would allow it to be used. I never saw it declined … And as soon as he'd sipped it, he'd nod his

Ann Whitmore (née Free) with her father, in front of 75a Histon Road.

head. And then we'd all rush forward and got our containers to be filled up with soup … and we'd get two loaves of bread … and we had as much soup as you could take. And it used to slop all over the Histon Road because we just had to carry it back from St John's College to Akeman Street, [where some of her family lived] … but it was beautiful soup. And interestingly … when meat became difficult to get hold of, the college owned lots of big houses and they used to have their own deer. And we actually had venison in the soup quite often because that was the only way of getting meat.

Ann remembers various local shops.

There was Mr Westrop's shop, which is now Headlines the hairdressers. And I suppose at the time we used to seem to go in there quite a bit, but it was wooden floors … it was only lit by gaslight. It was so dark in there anyway. But you'd go in there and there would be a smell of creosote and paraffin. And it was very dark. And his counter was very high. And you go in there and couldn't see anything hardly. And then suddenly, 'Can I help you?', and you'd look and he'd make you jump because this little … and he wasn't very big and his little head would pop up behind the counter … I can always remember that. But that was a sort of general hardware store. I can remember sort of what d'you call it – aluminium bars, buckets and balls and things like that there, and I think he did vegetables.

She also remembers Mr Phillips' shop opposite at 60 Histon Road.

My wedding bouquet was made by Bert Phillips, who kept the shop on Histon Road and also lived next door to me. And they were Bert and Bea and absolutely lovely friends and would do anything for us.

I realise now, of course, obviously they sold flowers because that would be useful for the cemetery, for people going to the cemetery to get the

Bert and his mother, Phoebe Phillips.

flowers. I don't know how long the Phillips family had that shop, but it was right … oh, it's so difficult today … things just aren't there. But it was on the corner of Bermuda Terrace. And it went down quite a little way because he had a sort of yard attached to it and it went round the corner. And he also got around the corner of the glass windows and he used to breed chickens. And there would be the lights on. The little baby chicks were all running around there. And I don't know why or what all that was about. As far as I know he never sold chickens to eat. You see, that was what they first went in for. They always sold wreaths and they always did the holly wreaths at Christmas time.

It was Mr and Mrs Phillips who owned the shop. Mrs Phillips was a large lady and she was … and dear Ernie, always singing, always humming away. But he was a bit under her thumb, she was quite a large lady. And my mum had all these coupons, but she hadn't gotten the money to use them, you know, make use of all of them. And Mrs Phillips liked mum, because she would buy butter and balance things off her. My mum was glad to have the money and glad for them to be used. And I can be certain my mum was quite popular for that.

F. Whitham & Sons, 48 Histon Road.

There was still activity within the floristry business in the 1960s, and people from all over the country wrote to the Phillips requesting wreaths for graves in the cemetery. There used to be a bowling green and quoit pits between his shop and the British Queen pub, an open space that is now filled with houses. One of their most regular customers was Mr L. J. Mynott, for some years a member of Cambridgeshire County Council. It was Mr Mynott who organised VE and VJ Day celebrations in the area and also a homecoming fund for the troops.

More grocers, fruiterers and florists were situated on Histon Road, and included F. Whitham at no. 48, G. J. Pilgrim, who was also a shoemaker, at no. 98, and W. A. Taverner at no. 169, not to mention wholesalers such as Ainger's Nursery, which subsequently became Scotsdale's, and Clive Vale Nursery.

F. Whitham & Sons belonged to the grandparents of Carole Jones, who still lives locally.

I am not sure exactly when they moved to the shop at 48 Histon Road, but working from significant dates in my father's timeline, I think it must have been around early 1930s and the photo would have been between then and 1934. The main shop was actually a two-storey house and the shop area was the front sitting room. I remember there was a door from the shop through to the family room at the back with kitchen and stairs to the three bedrooms above. There was a curtain over the door to the shop which I would peep round on visits to grandmother with my dad. Uncle Fred was not amused!

The business continued with just grandad, Fred and Ernest [Yallop] until grandad died in 1951. The wet fish shop carried on for a few more years but finally closed and Fred continued to run the fruit and vegetable side and gradually introduced other grocery products. Grandmother still lived at the back and upstairs until she died in 1961.

Fred continued with the shop but eventually retired and closed the shop for good around the mid '60s to the best of my knowledge and memory. The premises were sold and later became a ladies' hairdressers and I did have my hair cut there once as I was curious to see if any of my childhood memories were still there. Grandad and grandma are both buried, together, in Histon Road Cemetery.

Ann Whitmore remembers Yallop's fish.

Tiny little shop when you look at it now, it must be really small. I can remember it being small, but I used to be very friendly with Pat Yallop who lived … they lived in Akeman Street.

Bermuda flats

Kay Harris came to Cambridge in 1982 and, after working in retail for a number of years, became involved with the building of the Bermuda Flats Community Room, fundraising with residents via coffee mornings, car boot sales, raffles and applying for grants. The room was eventually opened in 2006 and she became the Community Room Manager. She tells us:

People were very supportive because they knew they're going to get a community room … it's for everybody. It's always been for everybody in Cambridge. It's quite a big room. You know, you get 40 people in here quite comfortably.

We do have jumble sales, clothes sales … And also, when they hire the room, their rent goes towards paying for things for people in the area. It's not just, you know … we have people coming down from French's Road. A couple of people from Histon Road and Linden Close.

The Bermuda Flats and Victorian terraced housing of Bermuda Terrace look out over Histon Road Cemetery.

Shops near Bermuda Terrace

Ann Whitmore remembers buying chips at Wesley's fish shop at 113 Histon Road, which is where Domino's Pizza is now.

We'd go get our two pennyworth of chips, and you'd queue all round and there would be big high tables and things and we'd all be all the way around then go outside sometimes. And there were two ladies and a man, I think, that ran it and we used to say, 'Have you got any fritters?' And it was all the bits that had come off the batter and they'd put them on one side. And we used to get a bagful of fritters, as we call them, for nothing. They give them to you.

The Frying Pan, Paul Pegasiou's fish and chip shop.

The fish and chip shop went through several ownerships, but Paul Pegasiou took it over at the end of 1982, opening for business on 5 January 1983, and ran it for 20 years, until July 2003.

Paul is another Histon Road trader who still lives locally. He explained that his reason for setting up as a chippie was because he didn't have to pay VAT. He opened for 30 hours per week including four lunchtimes and five evenings, always closing at 9 pm. Ever mindful of his neighbours, he knew that good customers would buy their fish and chips earlier in the evening, and although he was opposite the British Queen pub, he never courted the closing hour crowd. After selling the Frying Pan, Paul went on to work for Waitrose in Trumpington and eventually retired at the age of 73.

As his next-door neighbour Paul Brazier tells us:

There can be few people locally that did not recall him and his excellent food. He is a lovely man.

Paul Brazier believes that his house, no. 111, is the oldest documented residence on Histon Road within the boundary of Cambridge. The original handwritten deeds and documents date back to 1831. They are lengthy, large documents and very elaborate both in terms of content and appearance.

It is a fairly plain property with late Georgian style sash windows, open fireplaces and lovely wide elm floorboards. As owners we have tried to maintain and conserve the property true to its original style. It is very draughty and bloody cold in the winter … but we love it.

There were several laundries in the Histon Road area. Washing clothes was one of the hardest domestic tasks, involving fetching and heating well water, scrubbing items on washboards, rotating them with wooden 'dollies' and then squeezing them through a mangle. The earliest laundries such as Scotsdale's (see chapter 6) did this hand washing. The Stokesay laundry at 142 Histon Road was run by the Papworth brothers until 1940 when Arthur sold out to Frank, and by the '60s it was owned by the Midland Co-operative Laundry. Ann Whitmore tells us that her sister Mabel worked there because it was conveniently close to home and she could keep an eye on their mother who was often ill. The laundry was by then mechanised, but still used its own well water. The equipment included a pressing unit that could deal with 50 shirts an hour. In addition to standard laundry and dry-cleaning, they operated a bagwash service, which meant that items could be collected clean and dried but unironed, so saving the customer money. The introduction of domestic washing machines after the war gradually led to the demise of some of the laundries.

Where the petrol filling station is now was a four-storey Barnardo's home named Rock End Preventive and Training Home. Opened in 1897, it housed 18 girls aged from 15 to 22, who were trained in laundry and other domestic work by Matron Superintendent Miss Mary Annie Lewis.

Rock End, early 1900s.

Rock End was the final house in Histon Road until the development of the McManus Estate and other houses to the north. By 1974 the houses on both sides of the road had been assigned numbers all the way to the Cambridge City boundary where Cambridge Road starts today.

French's Mill

On the opposite side of the road we have a private road with no name that leads to French's Mill. Karina Cleland remembers coming across the Mill when she first moved here in 1974.

I was a bit taken aback at the area. I'm afraid that this area in the '70s was really not your nicest part of Cambridge. And I remember on Histon Road, as we drove towards Windsor Road and towards the McManus Estate, on the right-hand side was French's Mill, which was just derelict, derelict land. It was just rubbish.

Chesterton Mill, also known as French's Mill, was a wind-powered corn mill set on land known as 'West Field'. Michael French is a descendant of this family, but only came to live in Cambridge more recently, long after his family had left the city and the mill buildings had been sold off. Many of his relations are buried in Histon Road Cemetery, and Michael has become engrossed in its history since retiring. He tells us that William Beart, a maltster, acquired a plot on which he built a substantial smock mill in 1847. By 1881 the road leading to what is now Victoria Road was known as Occupation Road and by 1891 this had changed to the present name of French's Road.

William French acquired a lease on the mill and bought some of the surrounding fields. He obtained the freehold of the half acre containing the mill and buildings at public auction for £440 in 1850 after William Beart died. This is recorded as 'land with windmill, granary, stable and outhouses and a newly built cottage comprising a parlour, back kitchen, two bedrooms over, a wash house and other conveniences approached by a 20-foot road from Victoria Road and by a 12-foot road from Histon Road'. The mill provided flour to local bakers.

The business continued until 1956, when it closed. In 1967 parts of the property were compulsorily purchased for the construction of St Luke's School. The mill buildings were converted to offices in 1982 and 1985.

The south end of Histon Road has changed continuously over the years, and what we have captured here are memories that came up during our meeting sessions and with other people we talked to. We have no doubt left out many family and business histories, which we hope have not been forgotten but are yet to be revealed by family members and local historians.

French's Mill with the chimney of the steam engine added in 1868.

Mount Pleasant House, Castle Street, 1970s. Below: The same view in 2020.

From Castle Street to Willowcroft

In the last couple of years, the view looking south on Histon Road to Castle Hill has changed from a large office building to an imposing college accommodation block, both named Mount Pleasant House. Rosemarie Hutchinson, who lived at 67 Histon Road as a child, has vivid memories of this vista at the end of the 1950s and start of the 1960s.

I remember when at the top of Huntington Road there used to be a pub called the Wheatsheaf. And next to that was two cottages painted white. One of them was a hairdresser's because I used to have to go up there with my brother and he had his hair cut and I'd have to sit and just sit and wait.

This was actually Castle Street, and not yet Huntingdon Road, which started a bit further along with the doctors' surgery at no. 1. Next to the Wheatsheaf on the corner of Mount Pleasant was Dan Morley's petrol station, originally a Victorian house, and behind that a dip in the ground created by digging clay for bricks. There was a set of garages with wooden doors in that dip, where local people kept their cars before Huntingdon Road had a lay-by. The hairdresser was in a row of small 18th-century cottages on Castle Street with wattle and daub walls, similar to many others in Cambridge, such as those still left opposite Hertford Street at the beginning of Chesterton Road that belong to Magdalene College. There were many such buildings in King Street, a Cambridge style of house a lot of which have been pulled down.

The first street off Histon Road to the west is Canterbury Street. Karen Ready, who has lived in Benson Street, off Canterbury Street, since she was born, wondered what the true origin was of the naming of these side streets of Canterbury, Benson and Priory Streets. Mary Benson was a local landowner of many plots of land all over Chesterton parish, which included Histon Road and down to the boathouse areas on the River Cam behind Chesterton Road, and these can be seen on an enclosure map (p. iv) and accompanying ledger of 1840 at Cambridgeshire Archives. Benson Street first appears in Spalding's Directory in 1874, and Priory Street in the 1881 census, so must have been built shortly before these dates. Canterbury Street was originally named Canterbury Terrace and the seven houses on its north

This plaque may portray Edward White Benson (1829–1896).

side, now numbered 2 to 14, are shown in Spalding's Directory of 1884.

Coincidentally, Benson, Canterbury and Priory Streets might seem to commemorate E. W. Benson, Archbishop of Canterbury from 1883 until his death in 1896. Alison Hennegan lives at right angles to the end house on Benson Street, no. 26, and has always wondered:

Looking out of the window, I can see it affixed to the side of the first house on Benson Street, this interesting black plaque with a male profile with mutton chop whiskers and very pronounced nose, and a crown almost on the top of the circular plaque. And I have always wondered what that is. It's not unlike the profile of Edward White Benson, who became eventually Archbishop of Canterbury.

But how likely is it for an archbishop to have plaques, or wall ties, made in his image? And if not in his image, then whose? We have not found any family relationship between Archbishop Benson and Mary Benson. However, we still wonder whether the question about the plaques and date of the appearance of Canterbury Terrace might have coincided. Was there perhaps a conscious attempt to link Archbishop Benson's name with the area after 1883? Or perhaps this is no more than a fire mark, the uses of which ended around 1884.

At our public meeting covering the south end of Histon Road, in October 2019, local residents reminisced about Playfair Works, the sports factory on Benson Street, now replaced by Chamberlin Court flats.

At that meeting, Mahmood Mohammed Darr told us about his work as a foreman for Gray's and that he lived in Priory Street. Mahmood first came to Cambridge from Shalkot in Pakistan where his father manufactured sports equipment, including hockey sticks, traditionally made from the wood of local mulberry trees. Shalkot is a city steeped in sports equipment

Playfair Works from 14 Benson Street, by Jon Harris, 1986.

manufacturing, so it was not such a strange coincidence that Mahmood's father should sit next to Mr Gray on an aeroplane and they soon got into conversation. They eventually went into business together, and the Darr family came over to Cambridge to help run the factory.

David and Marion Keyworth who live on Benson Street, and Mahmood Darr, jovially reminisced about the activity at Gray's factory, including incidents in Benson Street itself. In our recording of their story, Marion started by telling us about the factory when they first moved there.

They used to have all these great delivery lorries that came down the road and stopped on the double …

And talking in the type of unison when one spouse finishes the sentence of the other, David continued:

David and Marion Keyworth. Below: Karen Ready in front of her house on Benson Street.

So this was about the cheapest street, this end of town. It was gravel, the road was gravel down the middle. Paving slabs represented the footpath … Yes, there were cobbles for about two feet, three feet out into the road. And then it was just gravel on the top, consolidated and then sprayed with tar. They broke the mains water and gas pipes which were situated close to the surface, more than once, causing untold mayhem with escaping water and gas.

The factory siren sounded at 8.15 a.m. to start the working day. David and Marion remembered the all-pervading smell of cellulose varnish, used to finish off the tennis rackets. David tells us:

You know, when we look out the window, seeing these tennis rackets trundling along on a sort of conveyor belt, you know, being done or having been done … And then as they were finished and dried, when they opened the windows, you could see them stringing the rackets. Prepared, you know, getting them ready, and then they were all wrapped up and went off to be sold. But they had to open the windows, otherwise, I think the workforce would have all passed out. Half, I mean, half the street did on a good day. On a good day we were all as high as kites.

Various local residents remember doing outwork for Gray's. Ann Whitmore remembers her aunt and another friend stitching toys at home.

Oh, that was the Gray's factory. That was Yvonne's mother. And yes, Gray's factory were making toys. And they … I remember these lovely fluffy lambs with real lambswool.

According to Mahmood Darr, the toys may well have been mascots sold alongside tennis rackets or hockey sticks.

Karen Ready still lives in the house on Benson Street bought by her father and grandfather in 1955. It had previously been a shop, hence the large front window.

Both Karen as well as David took photographs of Mr Gray landing a helicopter on the roof of Playfair Works, although by the time they had each got their cameras out the helicopter had all but disappeared over the roofline and landed. There was a rumour that the roof held a tennis court. With evidence that Mr Gray was building another floor on his factory, Karen's parents complained to the Council and the *Cambridge Evening News* printed the story.

Karen produced the newspaper cutting dated Saturday 9 June 1973, which says that Cambridge residents today accuse Gray's the sports equipment manufacturers of defying a Council order to stop work on a second storey extension to their Benson Street factory. The company had started work without planning permission.

> So my family is named as people complaining about this behaviour, and it includes 82-year-old Mrs Winifred Ready who was my grandmother, who is quoted here. I wonder if she had been at all pleased about her age going in the paper, but newspapers were prone … to want to know people's ages, and she certainly said how annoyed they were.

However, Mr Gray's methods were not all so dubious, and he was a generous employer. He allowed Mrs Powell to stay in a house belonging to Gray's on Benson Street after her husband who worked there as a foreman

Alison Hennegan supervising students, Canterbury Street.

died. A friend of Karen's lodged with Mrs Powell and fondly remembered his time there in the 1950s, and wrote to Karen.

He was a graduate student who lodged at number 25 at that period, and he lodged with a lady called Mrs Powell who rented the house from Gray's. She considered Gray's to be a very good employer and good to her as a tenant. She provided hearty breakfasts he says here, very hearty. But very friendly with her lodgers and he was friendly back and helped her doing some gardening and things like that. And, at that time of course they had no running water as such in his room, so she would bring up a large jug of water in the morning for him to wash and that sort of thing. So, I thought that was a nice little indication of how things were and of course in those days people had outside toilets and all sorts of things like that.

Mortgages

How does anyone ever afford a mortgage? Even though mortgages in the 1960s and '70s were allotted on a far lower income than today, this didn't necessarily make obtaining one any easier. Both Alison Hennegan and David Keyworth told interesting stories about how they gained their mortgages for their houses in Canterbury Street and Benson Street respectively.

Alison lives in what people call 'The Book House' in which she supervises university students and keeps many thousands of books. She bought her house in 1977 and tells us:

I had no job, which makes me a very unlikely person to be allowed to buy a house. But there was a company called C. C. Lee, which I think still exists [actually bought out in 2016]. Mr Lee has long since, I assume, gone to join the brokers in the sky, and permitted himself at least one silly human investment per year in the sense that he would use his considerable power to persuade the Cambridge Building Society to offer a mortgage to a, on the face of it, supremely unpromising person. And that year, for complicated reasons, I was that person.

It was okay structurally, anything that needed doing was cosmetic. But I had many thousands of books to move in. So, no 'cosmetisation' happened at all. And still hasn't. And so that's now 52 years later. We don't progress much.

David and Marion Keyworth bought their house on Benson Street in 1968 after he started working for Gerald Turvill at Scotsdale Nursery, at 299 Histon Road, and tells us:

I managed to get a mortgage by deceit because I was working for Gerald Turvill at Scotsdale's then and I didn't earn enough money. You got your mortgage in those days based on three times your salary, which was very sensible. And I didn't earn a thousand pounds a year then, which is inconceivable to think about now. I mean, that's what you expect to earn a month. So, Gerald, I went to Gerald and I said, 'Gerald, can you write me a letter, please, and say that I've been paid more than I have?' He said 'Well, I will, so long as you don't hold it against me.' So we went along and saw the mortgage manager, at the Abbey National as it was then, and he said 'Oh well, that's okay'.

North Street and Westfield Lane

Houses on the west side of Histon Road back onto North Street up until number 101 Histon Road, and are accessed from Canterbury Street. North Street runs parallel to Histon Road and used to be a quiet, leafy lane where neighbours stopped for a chat. Histon Road back gardens have been sold off for development over the last 25 years and now a distinctive set of modern buildings has been built. Pat and Tony Stokes' house on Histon Road has kept its long garden and garage, which still backs onto North Street.
Pat remembers:

North Street was a very quiet back street and our children used to play in it most days, all weathers. An American neighbour who was an author wanted to have it made into a traffic-free street for families with children to enjoy. This didn't happen as we had the park and a few residents with cars who needed to use the street.

The American author was the writer Charles Alverson, and the park, of course, was Histon Road Recreation Ground, commonly called 'the Rec'.

In North Street, our neighbour turned her garage into her sewing room; she was an excellent dressmaker and seamstress.

Westfield Terrace is a set of six houses at right angles to North Street, built in the 1960s, with garages set out in front facing North Street. Pat Stokes, who lives in Histon Road, remembers that it had previously been the site of a beautiful old house set in a spacious garden filled with cultivated blackberry bushes. She and her husband, Tony and their children picked an awful lot during the final autumn before the building began.

There is an entrance to the Rec from the end of Canterbury Street as well as on Histon Road. We have not been able to trace the opening date of this public amenity, but it is probably the patch of land indicated on a map in the *Cambridge Chronicle* of 1928 and had been orchards. It is captioned on Spalding's Map of Cambridge dated 1934. Gradually the Rec improved and in the '50s had a caretaker. Barbara Jago remembers:

There was a fella that used to be there all the time … the kids all used to call him Curly because he had curly hair … If any of the boys were larking about he'd probably give them a clip round the head – in those days – which you could.

Maureen Newman recalled that the gates used to be locked at 9 pm. There were not so many slides and swings as there are now and it needed more lights, but it was 'a nice park'.

Karen Ready spoke about the improvements.

The Rec is just marvellous these days. It's got all sorts of equipment, all sorts of areas, landscaping. Wasn't like that at all when I was a child [in the 1960s and '70s]. It was very rudimentary playing equipment. I don't think I spent much time on it to be honest. It was a little bit rough.

Karina Cleland remembers it in the 1970s as just a few cut-down trees. It wasn't used as much as it is today, and there is no longer any inkling of the 'rough' edge Karina mentions. The Rec is very popular with residents from this area of Cambridge.

Very recently the routes into the Rec have been delineated by wayfinders of flocking birds in bright colours, sitting on top of tall poles, which mark the entrance points on Histon and Richmond Roads, and Canterbury Street. The Friends of Histon Road Recreation Ground instigated this project to improve the entrances to the park. They commissioned the artists at the Dallas-Pierce-Quintero studio who worked with children on the project.

Histon Road Recreation Ground, commonly known as 'the Rec'.

They held a number of workshops in local schools, including Mayfield Primary School. The children explored the history of the Rec and helped to select themes to develop and chose the flocking birds design. The birds were chosen to reflect those that would have frequented the area at the time it was a tree nursery. The Rec is very popular and more lush, with many more trees than when our interviewees described it in their youth. You can also play table tennis on permanent tables. Ed and Rosie Zanders, who retired to Canterbury Street, regularly played there as part of their coronavirus lockdown exercise regime.

Adjoining the Rec, further down Histon Road, we come to a larger area that opens out north and south to accommodate Murketts' and ATS Euromaster, and backs onto Richmond Road gardens. This area had been known as Willowcroft and housed various industrial and semi-industrial companies, one of which was T. R. Freeman, founded in 1887 to carry out plumbing and roofing repairs for Cambridge University. A contributor told

us that he worked for them in the ’70s fitting central heating in the colleges. Freeman’s went from strength to strength, becoming a contractor to the Ministry of Works, War Office, Air Ministry and Local Authorities. The company moved to Waterbeach and one of its many projects was copper cladding for the Accordia housing development in Brooklands Avenue, which won the RIBA Stirling Prize in 2008. Sadly, it is now in administration.

In the 2006 Cambridge Local Plan, the designated use of the Willowcroft site was changed from industrial to residential. As this involves blocks of flats, it will add to the density of population in the area, though probably improve its appearance.

Aerial photograph of Histon Road Cemetery.

Histon Road Cemetery

A significant feature at the south end of Histon Road is the cemetery, which is an important resource when exploring the history of this area. It accommodates around 3,800 graves, and around 8,245 interments – although with only about 1,350 memorials.

The cemetery was created by the Cambridge General Cemetery Company Ltd in 1842–43, at the very edge of the town where only a few houses already stood, and is an example of a burial ground built during the great urbanisation of England, when families moved away from their rural roots, and into towns and cities. New graveyards were required as well as existing churchyards, to accommodate the larger number of burials of the growing urban population.

It was designed by John Claudius Loudon (1783–1843), an original and influential thinker who held pioneering views about the necessity of public open spaces within cities. Loudon designed Birmingham Botanical Gardens and glasshouses and the Derby Arboretum. Indeed, he was responsible for popularising his own professional description as a 'landscape gardener'.

Histon Road Cemetery included the Lodge at the Histon Road entrance, and a Gothic chapel in the middle with fine stained-glass windows, designed by Edward Buckton Lamb (1805–1869). It is included on the Register of Parks and Gardens of Special Historic Interest at Grade II as an early garden cemetery, designed for a provincial city, and laid out by Loudon. Although set up by non-conformists, people of all denominations were allowed a space, and the majority of people buried there had lived locally. It included those from all walks of life, both rich and poor.

In 2005, a group of committed volunteers was brought together by ward Councillors Rupert Moss-Eccardt, who lived in the Cemetery Lodge, and Anthony Hymans. From this initial meeting of local residents, the Friends of Histon Road Cemetery (FHRC) group was born. As a consequence, Liz Moon, Michael French and colleagues took on the formation of the Friends, and Liz related their story to us at one of our meetings.

Liz Moon.

I've lived on Bermuda Terrace since the early 1980s and I trained and worked as an engineer and then as a primary school teacher … At that time, the cemetery did not feel terribly safe. It was originally a greenfield site on the edge of Cambridge. I think it was owned by French's Mill, Michael French's family, and they sold it to the cemetery company in 1842 … so they ran it until 1936, and they ran it as a business and it was the non-conformists who built it. And it has most of the business people of Cambridge and their families, partly because if you were a non-conformist, you couldn't go to [Cambridge] university. So all these bright, clever people were actually creating Cambridge businesses rather than going off being academic. So, Cambridge benefitted, really.

Although it embodies Loudon's most important ideas on cemetery design, with its formal grid pattern layout and evergreen trees, Liz tells us that part of the business side of the cemetery, presumably at a later stage, meant they could sell flowers, and that there was a flower garden there and they would sell flowers on Sundays to families coming to see loved ones. The cemetery was looked after by a supervisor, or custodian, and kept beautifully. Liz tells us:

And then in the 1950s, the chapel was demolished. There's a funny story about that. We've heard this story from the lady who grew up in the Lodge and she said her mother heard bashing one day and rushed out to find somebody was destroying the chapel, and it wasn't meant to be. It was meant to be a meeting with the City Council to *discuss* destroying the chapel. She rushed in and saved as many of the memorials as she possibly could, including some from the Trumpington family, which she then took down to the family later. But it was this sort of madness that happened, rushing out and seeing ball and chain hitting it down.

The lady who grew up in the Lodge was Mrs Martin, whose husband was Custodian of the Cemetery from 1954 to 1959, and one of the memorials mentioned was a bust of Lord Pemberton. Liz continues:

In 1985 they came and dug up the old foundations of the chapel in the middle and planted holm oaks on that central island which have grown quite big, now surrounding a chestnut which is looking a bit sad. Then, I don't quite know when – I didn't notice – cost cutting happened. The gardener went, teams and hedge cutters were employed by the Council and the whole thing just completely got minimum care, hedges and bushes grew scuffed, tree skirts fell, haven for ASB [anti-social behaviour] drink, drugs, anything, whatever. Few local people went in. And I was glad of the spiky fence in front of my house. It gave me some sort of protection from what was going on out there. After a particularly distressing attack on my house, I wanted to move. There were teenage boys playing with an air pistol in the cemetery. They'd had it for Christmas or something. This is their big open space, and what they didn't know was the pellets, which went so far, broke my windows.

When the Friends of Histon Road Cemetery was formed, the City Council set aside £30,000 to contribute to the renovation of the cemetery. The Friends reformulated their aims and objectives. Using scissors and sticky tape they put together their Constitution – to protect and enhance the historic cemetery for public benefit as a place of remembrance, spirituality, history and nature. They then leafleted a wide area – not just the neighbouring houses that they were actually required to consult – asking residents their opinions about what they wanted from the cemetery. They also started to find out, bit by bit, who they could call on for help, both in terms of local resident volunteers as well as professionals within the Council. Liz continued:

Our first big spend of that £30,000 that was allocated to the cemetery was the questionnaire that went out in March 2007. An extensive consultation exercise was undertaken; we distributed 2,000+ questionnaires to local residents of which some 440 were completed and returned.

We discovered that the crematorium and 'Parks and Open Spaces' shared responsibility for the cemetery. Neither quite knew what the other was doing, which had possibly led to its deterioration. One day I saw a tree being cut down and nobody told us it was going to happen. Here he is, cutting down a rather large yew tree in the middle. And I ran to find out what was happening in that cramped and open space. Nobody knew. And that's when we discovered that there was the tree department as well within the Council that nobody had bothered to tell us about.

There was somebody in the Council who was responsible for memorial safety.

Steve Perry – he's the memorial safety person who had just been employed, actually, so for him it was a new job and he quite enjoyed looking around with us and looking at the memorials and deciding what was safe, what wasn't safe. If the memorials are sufficiently leaning, they become a safety hazard and we'll be funded by the Council [to rectify them]. If they're just leaning a little bit and dead and very beautiful, then it's not a Council responsibility. So, over the years, the Friends have donated funds which we've used especially for … memorial repairs. And that's been an ongoing project.

Of the vagrants who made use of the cemetery there was one man from 222 – a support centre in Victoria Road for the homeless, particularly those with addiction or mental health problems, and Liz tells us:

He looked like a giant gnome. He was tall and very rum, but he had a little hat and green clothes and he looked like he was enormous and he was a great sleeper-under-the-bushes. And I used to go and wake him up and say 'Come and do a bit of work'. 'No, no, I can't lose my unemployment benefit whatever'. But I said 'Well, it's charity work, you wouldn't lose anything'.

Liz encouraged volunteers in the various tasks necessary to pull the cemetery back into shape, and recognised that each volunteer was happiest when engaged in work that really appealed to them, and where they could get on with what they enjoyed. Michael French set to researching and writing histories for the Friends' newsletter and on open days he conducts tours of the graves. The first newsletter, printed in the autumn of 2007, contained news about the cemetery, photographs of the season and Michael's historical research into families buried there. Another volunteer, Rod Mulvey, has taken on the wildlife work and, with colleagues, put up bird and bee boxes, built insect fences, and collected examples of, and identified, all the different wild grasses that grow there.

The newsletters contain superb photographs of wildlife spotted in the cemetery, particularly butterflies and moths.

Local stories

There are many stories of individuals buried in the cemetery, and at our first meeting at the Bermuda Community Room, two Chinese men arrived unexpectedly, directed by Mike Petty whom they had originally contacted. They were looking for the grave, and descendants, of Dr Stephen Sturton, a missionary doctor who had saved the lives of around 1,000 civilian victims of the Sino-Japanese war of 1937 to 1945, at Hangchow Church Missionary Society Hospital, and helped another 2,500 refugees. Gradually, the singular story of this since-forgotten intern unfolded. According to Shi Weidong, an historian from Hangzhou University, Dr Sturton is considered to be the 'Schindler' of Hangchow (now called Hangzhou City). He wrote to Mike:

The reason why I'm interested in his research is that he had played an important role in our city local history. According to his autobiography *From Mission Hospital to Concentration Camp*, he was 'born at 6 Park Terrace, Cambridge, on 12 September, 1896, in a room overlooking Emmanuel College paddock'. His parents were Richard Sturton and Mary Emma. He later attended the Emmanuel College and became a surgeon. He married Rose Emmily Jelly [Emily Jelley] on 26 July 1921 and came to Hangchow on Christmas Eve to serve at Hangchow C.M.S Hospital. The hospital was mainly set up by Dr David Duncan Main in 1869.

C.M.S. refers to the Church Missionary Society. Shi Weidong continues:

> Dr Sturton devoted himself in humanitarian missions in China. He was engaged in the Chinese civil war against the northern warlords in 1928 and the 'Shanghai Incident' between China and Japan in 1932. He won medals from the Chinese government for his bravery in field hospitals … Furthermore, he was elected as the Secretary of International Relief Association to be in charge of relieving refugees. So, in one word, he saved the lives of wounded soldiers and another 25,000 refugees when our city was sacked to Japanese occupation. But this threw him into disaster that he was caught to the Japanese concentration camps in Shanghai and Peking after the Pacific War broke out.

Michael French had already researched the life of Sturton, and met the Chinese researchers by chance one day when cycling through the cemetery. They were beside Dr Sturton's grave, and Michael stopped to ask if he could help them. They exchanged stories about Sturton and Michael sent them his article.

Alison Wilson and Shi Weidong.

Stephen Sturton's headstone.

Personal stories of those buried in the cemetery

A cemetery is going to be full of remarkable and poignant stories that tell of world as well as local histories, and at Histon Road we have examples of both. The first thing that those of us who have lived in Cambridge for a while may recognise are names on headstones of notable families buried there – such as the drapers and shop owners Eaden Lilley, a family department store in Market Street, the Mitchams of Mitcham's Corner, and the Thodays who ran a fabric shop on St Andrew's Street where Santander and its neighbours are now.

Alison Wilson has also researched some of the names found on the graves.

I was surprised to find some well-known names in the cemetery – Mary Bateson for example. Since the 100th anniversary of women getting the vote we've heard a lot about the Cambridge campaigners. Mary was a medieval historian at Newnham College and joined the Suffragists, the less militant branch. She and her mother and sister Margaret (later Heitland) were all supporters and Mary became Secretary of the National Union of Women's Suffrage Societies. Her life was cut short in 1906 at the age of 41.

Francis Thoday (1826–1902).

Mary Bateson (1865–1906).

Alfredo Kanthack (1863–1898).

Horace Darwin, son of Charles, is described as the founder of the Cambridge Scientific Instrument Company, but a lot of the money behind it came from his friend at Trinity College, A. G. Dew-Smith, who inherited a fortune. He was a hands-on partner too, a lens maker and early photographer in the 1880s. He was buried in the cemetery in 1903.

Among other members of the University is Alfredo Kanthack, a Brazilian who became Professor of Physiology, although only for a year because he died in 1898 at the early age of 35.

For anyone interested in historical research, the cemetery opens up all sorts of avenues. There are hundreds of stories like this to be told, but not everyone buried in the cemetery is notable, of course, and it is full of the unmarked graves of children. Michael French tells us:

Of all the interments, some 1,500 are stillborn babies and infants under 1 and a further 952 are children between 1 and 12. These figures remind us of the high infant mortality in the late Victorian time. At the other end of the age range, there are seven centenarians.

Ann Whitmore tells us of her family who are buried there.

I was always told this is the aunt's grave and it was a double grave. And they said it was my aunt. I thought, being older people. But since then I've found when clearing out all of the photographs and things, I discovered that this was the grave of these four little babies. My mum's brothers and sisters that died when there was an epidemic of – I think it was measles, scarlet fever, or something like that. And they'd all died within a year of one another. And it was really tragic because the oldest one, I think, was five, and then it went four, three. And then there was a baby and this was the grave, and they were quite right. They were my aunts, but they were babies.

War stories

Dr Janet Bunker, Vicar in the Parish of the Ascension, has commemorated the 170 men inscribed on a World War I memorial at St Luke's Church, for the anniversary of the end of the war in 1918, including those buried

The Cemetery Lodge.

at Histon Road Cemetery. There is always a gathering at the cemetery on Remembrance Sunday and again, Michael French researched those who died in war, and are either buried or commemorated at the cemetery. According to Michael, there are 36 graves that relate to young men who lost their lives in World War I. There are 12 burials, 6 in family graves and 6 marked by Commonwealth War Graves Commission headstones. A further 24 young men are remembered on family graves. Of these, 10 are buried in CWGC cemeteries in France and Belgium, and 14 have no known grave.

The Cemetery Lodge

Not all cemetery stories are so hidden, or so sad, and the ambience lightens when Ann Whitmore goes on to tell us of her friendship with Yvonne Pryor whose father was superintendent of the cemetery from 1935 until 1947. Ann lived at 75a Histon Road.

And my dearest friend, and she still is, bless her. It was Yvonne Pryor. She lived at the … across the road, at the cemetery, in the cemetery lodge. Yvonne and [I] … Histon Road Cemetery was our playground. And we used to have some marvellous games and things in there, with the little chapel in the middle.

It was also the ARP [Air Raid Precautions] post, and so it had a telephone. Nobody had telephones in those days. And I remember Yvonne's mum and dad went out one evening and they said jokingly, they said, we didn't realise … they said, if anybody rings up, tell them I've gone to see a man about a dog. And sure enough, the phone rang and Yvonne said, 'No, mummy and daddy have gone to see a man about a dog'. We were quite disappointed that they didn't bring the dog.

Ann suffered the kind of accidents so common with young children playing together where they shouldn't.

I fell back onto one of these glass memorials. And I was bleeding quite badly. And I had to go over to my aunt and she put me in a bath.

The cut was very deep and Ann's aunt wanted to take her to the hospital, but Ann cried out:

I'm not going to the hospital. I'm not gonna let anybody see this cut! And then Yvonne, naughty … about a week or so later, she said to me, 'That lady's been round to see who broke her vase'. I said, 'Oh', you know, I was really frightened, I thought she was going to come and tell me off, but she was just teasing me. But yes, Yvonne and I, we met when we were 5 years old and we are now both 84 and we are still the best of friends. And we still see each other regularly. And we've been on lots of holidays around the world together. And I was her chief bridesmaid.

After Mr Martin left the cemetery, there was no one person to care for it, and the Lodge was rented out. Charles Alverson bought it when the Council decided to sell, around 1980. Charles was a Californian who had settled in Cambridge. He was a writer, and besides having written for the *Wall Street Journal* while living in San Francisco, also indulged his inimitable sense of the absurd by writing for the Monty Python team after migrating to the UK. He tells us, albeit in the third person:

After five happy years living in mid-Wales, Alverson moved to Cambridge, England. There he continued to write novels (two of which were published over nearly 15 years, which ain't much of a record) and wrote two films (*Jabberwocky* and *Brazil*) with Gilliam. Actually, he wrote only the first draft of *Brazil*. He also got divorced again [for the second time] but moved only across the street into a cemetery lodge.

While living there, Charles met his soon-to-be third wife, Zhivana, and moved to her home city Belgrade 'doing hack journalism, teaching high school and doing damn-all writing' and then to a smallholding in Vojvodina in the north of the country in 2000, where he started writing fiction again. He had wanted to write us something of his time at the Lodge to share at our meeting, but suffering increasingly from Parkinson's disease he was unable to type. Very sadly, Charles died in January 2020, within a week or so of our second Bermuda meeting.

Charles is worth remembering as a man of true community spirit. He was a school governor, and a broadcaster on Addenbrooke's Hospital radio. He had the gift of the gab. When you visit Alverson's website a message scrolls across from right to left to say 'CONGRATULATIONS' and that 'you are the one millionth person to visit the website TODAY'. If you were to visit the website a year later, you would see the same message. So, now you really start to get the measure of Charles Alverson – full of energy, very kind, and great fun. The website contains several of Charles' writings – some excerpts from his novels and short stories, and a biography full of misdemeanours and journalistic experiences. They are all well worth reading.

The Friends of Histon Road Cemetery goes from strength to strength. It is very well run and holds open days, occasionally with activities such as local letter carvers who demonstrate the creation of lettering inscriptions on headstones, and with an active wildlife project. Although Loudon's design was formal, with its equal-sized quadrants cutting the graveyard north-south and east-west with gravel paths, and with light plantings of evergreen yews, he would surely be interested and appreciative to see how local people alongside the Council have come together to take on the care of the graveyard today.

All indications are that the cemetery is a highly valued green space in a densely built-up area. The Friends' Chairman, Alan Levy, encourages us to make use of it: 'The cemetery remains open, and for those of you living within walking distance it's an excellent place to visit as part of a daily exercise regimen'.

IN LOVING MEMORY OF
JOHN GOLDSMITH,
WHO FELL ASLEEP DECEMBER 22ND 1905
AGED 90 YEARS.
MARY GOLDSMITH,
NOVEMBER 11TH 1909
AGED 84 YEARS.
ALEXANDER MACINTOSH GOLDSMITH
APRIL 11TH 1901.
AGED 35 YEARS.

Council houses on Histon Road at the junction with Akeman Street.

Post-war development

The situation in 1945

In post-war Britain, there was an urgent need for more housing. Cambridge had suffered bomb damage to over 1,000 houses; much of its housing stock was old, and some quarters could only be described as slums. Added to that was the requirement to house evacuees from the London bombing. Planners looked to the edges of the city for development sites, Histon Road being one of those areas with plenty of open space.

There were already council houses off Histon Road in Akeman Street and Darwin Drive, built in the 1930s. Ann Whitmore's family grew out of their terraced house and moved to the council estate.

My mother got a council house in Akeman Street, the top end of Akeman Street, a four bedroom one. But even so, there wasn't room for me and my sister. Not really. Not comfortably. And so we stayed with the two aunts in Histon Road, and the two aunts worked at Chivers … So every morning they used to get me up and I would walk down to the end of Akeman Street and the bus, the Chivers bus would come pick them up and I would go on to my mother. And she would give me my breakfast and she'd do my hair and send me to school and I was then going to Milton Road School. So it was quite a long walk from Akeman Street to the end of Gilbert Road to Milton Road.

This development was not well built and had outside toilets. The Council attempted to upgrade it in the '80s by bolting on bathrooms to the kitchens, but this was not very successful so the houses were refurbished again in 1987. In 1933, the *Cambridge Evening News* reported that Cambridge was well ahead with its slum clearance scheme, and the following year the Mayor opened the 2,000th council house, situated in Bateson Road. Pre-war there was much private building too, in Gilbert Road, Gurney Way and Courtney Way, and in 1937 an advertisement stated that the 'Windsor Estate' was being rapidly completed. To the north, construction began in 1931 on a new road to join Milton and Histon Roads, described by the *Cambridge Evening News* as providing 'exceptionally attractive sites for those wishing to erect a private house'. This was King's Hedges Road.

Prefabs in Gilbert Close. Below: Mr Beeton, the milkman, giving a ride to a boy from the prefabs.

Prefabs and Borrowdale

The first social housing after the war was prefabricated and only intended to last 10 years. These 'prefabs' made of asbestos sheets could be erected in about 40 hours. The first to be constructed in our area were ready in September 1945. There was a set of 40 at Gilbert Close, starting just beyond the Langham House flats, with a footpath leading to Hurrell Road at the back, and a similar complex of 35 in Roseford Close on the other side of Roseford Road. Carole Jones and her daughter moved into a prefab opposite Carisbrooke Road in 1966 and stayed until 1971. She writes:

The prefabs were set out in rows of four and all had good sized gardens, front and rear, and all detached. They were made of asbestos which meant you couldn't attach anything to the walls. Mine had a particularly large garden, and benefitted from a concrete slab where you could park a car … There was a concrete coal bunker in the back garden.

The house was compact, convenient and well equipped, as Carole describes.

The prefab was very well designed and had a very efficient coal fire with a back boiler which heated the water, and there was a system of air vents which fed warm air to the bedrooms and hall. The kitchen was equipped with a built-in fridge and cooker and a large storage cupboard, and was large enough for a small table and chairs … The living room was big and so were the two bedrooms. The hallway was wide with an airing cupboard, separate toilet at the end and a decent sized bathroom. [It was] warm, comfortable and cheap to run.

Many tenants loved them and were reluctant to move out when the time came. The last were not demolished until 1972. Barbara Jago tells us:

Well they were there a long time. Longer than they were forecast to be – they started at Gilbert Road … And they were there for a long time after the war.

Maurice Beeton remembers his father delivering milk there in the '50s. Pictured is his Chivers' milk float near Roseford Close. Maurice himself followed in his father's footsteps.

Marion MacLeod outside her flat in Gilbert Close.

I was a milkman for Unigate and my round started at Murketts', top of Histon Road and I had over a 100 customers before I got to Akeman Street. This was in the '60s and '70s, so many memories; first milkman on McManus estate … Very happy days and what stories.

After clearing Gilbert Close, the Council built Borrowdale on the site, a mixture of flats on two levels and some houses. Marion MacLeod worked at Fitzwilliam College and was very pleased to be offered one of the flats.

It was very light both back and front. It was near to where I worked and near the shops and because I'm quite badly sighted I don't drive and I'm pretty well a hazard on a bicycle so I needed … it couldn't have been a better location really. After I moved I met some of the neighbours and they all seemed very pleasant.

It's one bedroom with a smallish but adequate kitchen and bathroom and it has quite a large boxroom, which is absolutely splendid, very good storage space and I think very well designed. It happened that a few years ago I met through somebody I was working with at the charity shop – I met her husband [Mervyn West] who turned out to have been the Council architect who had designed the Gilbert Close and Borrowdale flats in the 1970s when the Council did employ architects and to very high standards and I said to him, 'I think it's brilliantly designed'.

Lucy Cavendish College, graduate accommodation.

Marion has lived there over 30 years. She feels strongly about the 'Right to Buy' council housing policy:

> I could have just about managed the mortgage for my flat, but I thought, if somebody had bought my flat before me I wouldn't have got it, so I was really, really anti the 'buy your own council house'. It's really annoying.

Richard Newcombe Court, housing for older people.

The Council also built the complex of flats behind Bermuda Terrace. This had been the site of a foundry established in 1872 and the lane at the side was Foundry Road until renamed Bermuda Road in 1900. The addition of a Community Room is mentioned in Chapter 2.

It is notable that buildings added in the 21st century, often by demolishing what was originally there, all aim for greater population density. The main examples are Nido, student flats at the junction with Huntingdon Road; the stylish Lucy Cavendish College flats at 100 Histon Road; Richard Newcombe Court, with 40 'affordable' flats for older people; and Lawrence House, the tallest building in the neighbourhood, which replaced 2 houses with 13 apartments.

Langham House flats, refurbished with added penthouse, 2015.

The vanishing rural scene

Before the war, ribbon development spread down Histon Road away from the town centre. Plots in both Gilbert Road and Roseford Road were laid out in 1929, but not all the houses had been built when war broke out. The Art Deco style 1930s flats at the junction of Histon and Gilbert Roads were an exception to the detached family houses on the other plots.

Immediately after the war, this junction marked the end of built-up Cambridge apart from the temporary prefabs and a few outlying houses and Roseford Road. Remaining spaces in the top part of the road were soon filled in during the '50s, resulting in a mixture of styles. But driving out of Cambridge, allotments and orchards still flourished, and there were fields of corn around Roseford Road, extending across to Milton Road. Robin Barrett recalls a beekeeper with lots of hives on the west side, benefitting from the abundant blossom.

Rosemarie Hutchinson described the edge of town.

Where Aldi and Iceland is, that was just wilderness, it was just nothing. I remember McManus, Warwick Road and all the houses round there. I remember when that was just nothing … It was just trees and hedges and shrubs and stuff like that. We used to play cowboys and Indians. And further up, it was just – I mean going to Histon was just like a day in the country because there was no buildings or … Now we've got Orchard Park. You know, and every time we go past, I can smell those pigs, yeah pigs.

A lot of people kept pigs on their allotments, especially during the war when meat was scarce.

Barbara Jago, who was brought up in a three-bedroom house on Histon Road, has a long memory, and described the appearance of the whole area after the war.

You see none of these houses in Histon Road, on this side of the road, from where the shops are there was nothing there – no buildings at all on this side. At the far end [of Histon Road] there used to be a field with usually a couple of horses in and people had pigsties there.

When I started school at Milton Road School [mid-fifties] not all of Milton Road was built up – there was lots of gaps in the houses. There was Stretten Avenue came up to Gilbert Road and then Gilbert Road was a T-junction you know … there was no road opposite – that Carlton Way wasn't there. And there was one or two gaps … on both sides of the road. And just about where Carlton Way is … I seem to remember there was a thatched cottage stood quite a way back from the road [one of Hall Farm buildings] and I know that the chimney sweep lived there … And as a child I thought it was a lovely cottage. 'I'd like to live there' you know – a sort of fairy-tale cottage.

She remembers picking blackberries on the unoccupied plots of land.

The McManus Estate

The character of Histon Road was altered by two large building projects beyond the Gilbert Road junction. The first, beginning in 1947, was the Council development from Roseford Road to Arbury Road, which will be covered in a separate chapter. The second and more prominent one happened 12 years later when the Council allotments between Histon Road and Windsor Road were sold to a developer, the McManus company, for £4,500 an acre. An article in the *Cambridge Evening News* in September 1960

FOR VALUE IN CAMBRIDGE . . .

ON THE

CHESTERTON ESTATE

HISTON ROAD

Offering early occupation. Spacious 3-Bedroom Terraced Houses (as illustrated) with attractive tile-hung elevations. Two alternative interior arrangements are available. Type SE with 22ft. 9in. through Living Room, Type NE with "L" shaped Living and Dining areas. Both designs have open fireplace fitted back boiler, excellent Kitchen, Bathroom and W.C. In-built Fuel Stores. Garages available nearby if required.

Freehold Price £2,895 and £2,995

A DECORATED SHOWHOUSE IS AVAILABLE FOR INSPECTION, FITTED WITH CENTRAL HEATING IN THE FORM OF SAGER TANGENTIAL FLOW FAN HEATERS.

Spacious Detached 2-Bedroom Bungalows (as illustrated) featuring attractive Entrance Hall, 16ft. 9in. x 12ft. 6in. Living Room, well designed Dining/Kitchen 11ft. 6in. x 9ft. 3in., Bathroom and W.C. Garage Space.

Freehold Price £3,395

Semi-Detached 2-Bedroomed Bungalows (as illustrated) with good sized Living Room, well fitted Kitchen, Bathroom and W.C. Garage space.

Freehold Price £2,695

MAXIMUM MORTGAGES AVAILABLE

Full details available from:—

MC MANUS SALES OFFICE

HISTON ROAD, CAMBRIDGE *Telephone* CAMBRIDGE 57870

reported that McManus 'have decided to put up terraced houses rather than the traditional semi-detached properties on their projected estate ... They call it an experiment in contemporary living that can accommodate the same number of families but with a greater amount of space around the houses for children to play on'. By 1963 these were selling for £2,895, and they had broadened their offering to include detached houses and semi-detached bungalows.

McManus had built 400 housing units by 1969, when they decided to leave Cambridge after a disagreement with the Council about commercial development of the remaining unbuilt land bordering Histon Road. It was felt that this would provide too much competition for the existing shops. The developers made a huge profit on the land by selling six acres for £100,000, nearly four times what they had paid for it.

McManus were true to their promise of leaving plenty of open space round the houses, and this adds considerably to the quality of life on the estate. There are only two through roads, Carisbrooke and its subsidiary Tavistock, and all the rest are cul-de-sacs. Few of the roads are straight; they have pleasing curves, which forces any traffic to slow down. Alison Wilson moved to Holyrood Close in 2014.

It's quieter here than where I lived before [Leys Avenue] and everybody remarks on it. I think it's because I'm shielded by a number of roads which are not terribly busy. I can hear the A14 in the morning but I don't hear Histon Road – that's amazing – perhaps I will when they start doing roadworks. Holyrood Close is very quiet because it's in a cul-de-sac of course. You get very little traffic coming along.

Many of the roads were planted with grass verges and trees and several little pathways were left as shortcuts for pedestrians. Jo-Anne Kocian explained:

I used to go round Fontwell Avenue because there are passages adjoining Carisbooke Road into Fontwell and through from Fontwell into Tavistock Road where my grandparents lived. So we used to walk around there. And the green of course, adjacent to Mayfield School, that had always been there but that didn't have trees on it then; it was just grassed up. So children used to play football on it and games of football and cricket on it so that was a true summertime memory.

Advertisement for McManus houses.

Some of the houses in Lexington Close were actually owned by Cambridge Water Company, about three or four of them on the right-hand side going down. And also Stratfield Close was later built as well – joined on to Tavistock Road – and three or four of their houses were owned by Cambridgeshire Constabulary; they were police houses.

Finally, Belmore Close was built around 1970 on the wasteland next to Histon Road, but shielded from it by a belt of trees that mitigate traffic noise and pollution.

Jo-Anne lived in Lingholme Close with her mother from 1964.

She was happy here. I know she liked the estate because of the convenience of the shops – again we never had a car so it was walking everywhere for us and she liked walking along Histon Road because it was very pleasant then. There was an orchard, apple tree orchard, I think part of it is still there actually on this side of the road … And they kept geese in it so we both used to go for a walk there especially when I had my dog as he used to love walking along there watching the geese.

And down the side road behind the end of Tavistock Road there used to be a squash court and a laundry down there and at the end of that road was a riding school and a stables … And they used to come onto the estate, the riders, and that was quite nice to hear them trotting around. That was very pleasant, especially Sunday afternoons … And I always remember one Christmas when I lived in Chatsworth Avenue, they – the riding school – came bearing lanterns and they were singing carols. That was really nice. And as they were coming round it started to snow so that was absolutely beautiful – yes, really enjoyed that.

Terry and Janet Dunn also commented on the children's cricket and tennis matches on the green or in the cul-de-sacs where there was very little traffic. The Dunns bought their house in Lingholme Close a year and a half after getting married, moving from a caravan in Histon in 1971. At that time it was not difficult to get a big mortgage and they feel sorry for today's young people who don't have the same possibility to buy rather than rent.

Well it was great actually, because round here they were all young couples in the same situation as we were. They … we all had children round about the same time, great fun. The kids grew up. They all played together on the green, everywhere. Everybody was friendly with everybody … there was a lot of Tupperware parties, Pippa Dee [fashion sales] parties – used to go to other people's houses … And both boys, our two boys, both born in the house. Yeah, both born at home. A local midwife came in.

But we got highly involved in local [affairs] … Terry was on the committee at Mayfield, at the parent teacher association … And the cubs was run from St Augustine's.

The main thing was Mayfield fête. You got involved in that. I mean, you know, you raised a thousand pounds.

Terry: So that was a lot of money. There were a lot of good people on the PTA, and they were able to get raffle prizes off of local communities. It was a big thing.

Janet and Terry mentioned the convenience of the shops on Histon Road and the number of firms delivering to the door.

Terry: A chap come in selling eggs every Friday, lovely eggs.

Janet: And he used to do some cockerels at Christmas, didn't he, 'Would you like a capon?'

Terry: I know … the milk delivery was another thing.

Janet: Oh … the women on this estate loved Maurice, the milkman. Great big friendly man.

Terry: And of course as well you would get a delivery of coal, for the coal fire … there's someone coming round selling fish as well.

Janet: You got your weekly groceries in the Co-op and a nice lady there wrote your address on the bag of sugar and about three o'clock in the afternoon an old Co-op lorry used to turn up with your box of groceries and it used to belch diesel. It was a terrible old lorry, but it used to come. That used to be a feature when we first came here.

Several residents saw the shops as a focus for the community. Jo-Anne Kocian said:

You would always meet the neighbours and very often stop and have a chat – and I still do. I often have a gossip in the Co-op.

As a small child, her mother took her to the shops in the pram and left her outside.

That shows how times have changed.

Norma Davies did this too.

We had big prams, not the little ones like we have today, that were really big prams and we could put them on the front outside International Stores and they'd be safe. You put your brake on your pram and it would be amazing. And you never feared, you met all the other mums up there. And it was like our little outing.

She also went in the other direction, to the Post Office in Richmond Road and Wright's bread shop in Halifax Road, which sold tempting cream buns.

Karina Cleland moved into Tavistock Road a decade later in 1974. Her first impression was that Histon Road was 'a bit dilapidated', particularly around French's Mill, but she did appreciate 'nice shops, nice trees and just nice to live'.

So it had all the amenities. And I must say, the shops and the whole area has gone up a lot, hasn't it? Much nicer: love all the new buildings …

The shops were a good place to meet people, but a more important focus for the community was Mayfield Primary School, one of the first buildings erected by McManus on the site and opened in 1962. Its name was an acknowledgement of the rural area it replaced, 'May' being the hawthorn flowers in the hedges round the allotments. It became the centre for local activities such as clubs, meetings and parties.

Karen Ready remembers going to school there when it was newly built and smaller than it is today. She contrasts an old-fashioned maths teacher who humiliated children who couldn't answer his questions by sending them to the back of a line, with a more progressive one, Mr Cornwall.

He tried out new methods which often included drama about projects we were doing. It was very projects-based, which was a very '60s thing I know. So we would do dramas about the gods of China and something to do with Greece I think we did … the costumes were usually pillow cases that you cut out so you got arms. So everyone was wearing something standard – a pillowcase thing – and we made papier mâché masks, and I've probably still got one of those.

This teacher also mixed up the class to prevent little cliques developing.

You would be in little groups at tables and then periodically you would have to move round so that you met a new group of pupils.

Karen didn't realise at the time that it was a good idea: she wanted to sit with her friends!

Mayfield schoolchildren in the '70s.

Norma Davies appreciated the education her children received at Mayfield and later gave something back.

Well I have done voluntary work up there, and I have helped him with the computers up there for some time, and I helped in the dinner, the dinner time up there. I've always had a great fondness for Mayfield School because both my children went there and one of them is doing very well in dancing. And the other one, he owns a company in Sudbury.
And the grandchildren obviously have done extremely well. I've got a Cambridge graduate and an engineer, so school has been very good to us.

Karina Cleland was also very happy with it in the '70s.

Schooling was of course lovely because we were very spoiled with Mayfield School and living in Tavistock Road. We could just walk up to Mayfield School with my then four-year-old little boy. And Mayfield School had a lovely reputation, was a lovely school. And the headmaster was, he was very interested in football, but also in choir. And we actually had a choir, which was lovely. Yes. We rehearsed the *Messiah*.

Rosemarie Hutchinson found it convenient to work there when her daughters were pupils. Compared with St Luke's, where she was at school, it seemed very modern.

Tree-hugging in Histon Road.

I got a job at Mayfield School in the canteen serving the dinner … but yeah, it was nice seeing the girls play with their friends and I made friends with the other women.

In the present day, Mayfield is still a much-loved school with a good Ofsted report, and as a result of a fire in 2004 its internal arrangement and outdoor play areas have been considerably improved. Architecture students from the University planned the grounds as an exercise, consulting the children about what they would like. The school is enhanced by its surroundings, the green spaces outside the school boundary and tree-lined Histon Road.

Community

There are still quite a number of people on the McManus Estate who have lived there all their lives, like Jo-Anne Kocian in Lingholme Close who lives next door to Barbara Jago whom she knew as a child.

She used to take me out and about. Used to take me to the Cattle Market on Cherry Hinton Road when that was there … yes and the neighbours across the road, I grew up with their children which was nice because we both, all, went to Mayfield together.

Jo-Anne considers it 'a very community-spirited area' and gives the example of a sudden flood in the late '60s when she and her mother were living in Chatsworth Avenue.

We had a very heavy thunderstorm and a cloudburst and Lexington Close and Chatsworth Avenue became flooded, quite deeply flooded. And the water was swirling around our maisonette in Chatsworth Avenue … We just saved it actually just before the water got into the doorsteps. We were in the ground floor maisonette and my mother and I started bailing the water with buckets to save it just going in. When the neighbours came home from work they saw us struggling so they got some buckets as well and they formed a chain so that they were bailing water for us.

Neighbours sit out on the benches and chat in the summer and invite each other for coffee or tea. Many of them belong to the Seniors Club, which has met at the school once a month since 2009. The idea came from one of the schoolchildren, Ola Anderson.

Although most of the properties now, a lot of the properties are rented out but there's still the original folk that live here like me who have been here most of their lives. So we still all know each other and some people say 'Oh I've known you since you were a little girl Jo-Anne'.

Barbara Jago also appreciates the community cohesion. She has two really close friends on the estate and visits quite a lot of others.

When I was in hospital a few, a few years back both of them came every single day to see me. Now that takes a chunk out of your day in the afternoon. Apart from the difficulties of parking at the hospital – nice and expensive. And you know, when I came home, my fridge had been filled up. And one friend … looked after my dog while I was in hospital. And then for two or three weeks after I came home, she came round every day to take the dog out for a walk … and her husband came round to cut the grass while I was in the hospital.

Many residents would echo Jo-Anne Kocian when she says 'Yes – it is very much my area – my manor as they say in London'.

Over: McManus Estate from the air.

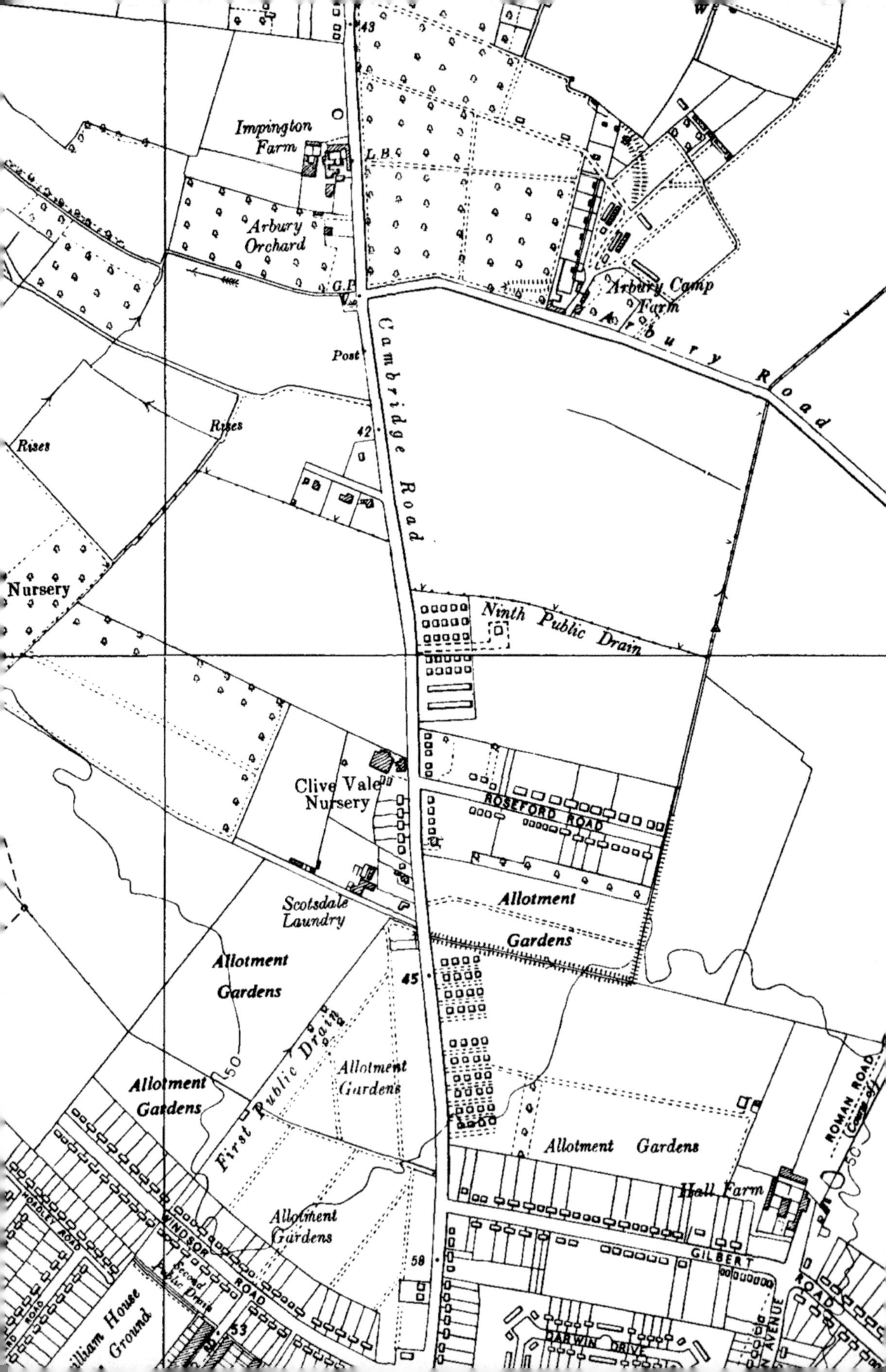
Impington Farm
Arbury Orchard
Arbury Camp Farm
Arbury Road
Cambridge Road
Post
Rises
Nursery
Ninth Public Drain
Clive Vale Nursery
ROSEFORD ROAD
Allotment Gardens
Scotsdale Laundry
First Public Drain
Allotment Gardens
Hall Farm
GILBERT
ROMAN ROAD
WINDSOR ROAD
HOADLEY ROAD
DARWIN DRIVE
AVENUE
Second Public Drain
William House Ground

From Gilbert Road to the northern boundary

Nineteenth century: Ainger's Nursery

Beyond Gilbert Road one of the oldest houses in the northern part of Histon Road, probably dating from 1860, is today numbered 312. It was originally called Providence House. The present owner, Molly Sneddon, told us its fascinating history and a family story that was only fully uncovered after World War II.

It was built by someone called George Tredgett from Bottisham who married a Miss Harvey. Ebenezer Tredgett [his son] is our main link to

Below: Providence House, Histon Road.

this house. He was born in 1847. And he wasn't a very happy schoolboy, and at age 13, he ran away to sea. He went to London, joined a sailing ship of the East India Company and was employed as a deck boy. The ship's master wrote to his father, asking permission to employ him as he was so young. The father wrote back. 'You can keep him. I don't want to see him again.'

However, Ebenezer came back to Cambridge after a few years and at the age of 19 married Sarah Careless in the Eden Chapel in 1866. They lived at Providence House, which then had a large garden fronting the road. He worked hard to build up a nursery, advertising in newspapers and exhibiting in local flower shows, usually winning first prize for roses and displays of pot plants and cut flowers. In 1873 he added his father's established seed business to his portfolio and called himself 'nurseryman, fruiterer and seedsman'. At some point he took on more land across the road, and by 1881 he was employing nine men and three boys. Molly continued:

He worked as a nurseryman and sold produce in a shop in Market Hill. Ebenezer and Sarah produced 10 children. He abandoned his wife and family in March 1885 when he left Cambridge. He sailed from Gravesend to New Zealand with Maude, who was Maude Constable, [his shop assistant] aged 20 years old. He left his wife and family and his wife, Sarah, took over the nursery business and ran the shop in Market Hill, changed the name to S. Tredgett and Sons.

Soon after Ebenezer left her, Sarah moved to 297 Histon Road, set back up a long drive and adjacent to the nursery. It was said to have been built by either Ebenezer or his father, who was a builder. It was then called Ainger Cottage.

An interesting detail is that Ebenezer sold his fine collection of 3,000 standard and dwarf roses at auction on 14 February 1885, a month before he emigrated, probably to finance the journey.

The story was discovered when an ex-neighbour of Ebenezer worked as a deck [hand], a crew member on the ship that Ebenezer and Maude travelled to New Zealand on. He wrote he recognised Ebenezer and Maude and reported the story to the *Cambridge Independent Press* as a sensation.

Ebenezer and Maude lived well on board as a married couple, and it was stated that his wife was in an interesting condition, I remember that.

They arrived in New Zealand in Auckland in 1897 and started another wholesale and auctioneering business from a small fruit shop in Auckland. A daughter was born, but sadly died at six months old. They went on to produce nine sons. The family worked hard. They flourished and they were well respected … They became committed Baptists. After Sarah died, in 1905, Ebenezer married Maude.

George and Mary Ann Tredgett, Ebenezer's parents, and Sarah, his first wife, are all buried in Histon Road Cemetery. Ebenezer, who had changed his name to Edward Turner in New Zealand, died in Auckland in 1918. Some say that his ghostly footsteps were afterwards heard at the nursery.

It was nearly a century later that his New Zealand descendants discovered the original Cambridge family. Molly said:

We have since received numerous members of the family who come to look at … their original home and they're still very interested in the garden and things that are planted in it. And we like to see them when they come.

When the Sneddons were bringing up their family there was a footpath across the fields past no. 297. Molly's husband used to walk across to NIAB (National Institute of Agricultural Biology) where he worked.

And we could walk up through; there were horses in the fields. In fact, I think one of our children had some horse riding lessons early on.

In another field there were cattle owned by Love's butchers in Histon. Avril Dring who lived at 301 described a 'leafy driveway off Histon Road, bordered on the south side by greengage trees and a brook', and Robin Barrett says that the brook reappeared on the other side of the road. It must have been one of the many public drains in the area.

Twentieth century: Scotsdale Nursery

Seventy years after George Tredgett started Ainger's Nursery the site was bought by Dudley Turvill, a mechanical engineer. As manager of the Swiss Laundry in Cherry Hinton Road he was primarily interested in the small Scotsdale Laundry at no. 301, but in 1958 an entry in the company's books reads, 'The house and land adjacent to the Scotsdale Laundry, known as 299, had been purchased for £2,000. The land behind 299 was to be cleared and handed over until needed by the company to Gerald Turvill as a nursery'. So it seems that this was brought into the Swiss Laundry's portfolio, while allowing Dudley's son Gerald to set up a business with his new wife Rosemary, who also worked at NIAB as a seed analyst. Rosemary writes:

We began with chrysanthemums, then progressed to unusual perennials, along with bedding plants. We lived at 299 Histon Road – a charming tiny house … We used mobile greenhouses – quite amazing – they were glasshouses on tracks, and we would grow chrysanthemums outside all summer in the ground, then push the greenhouses over them to protect the flower crop for the winter. Not to be seen these days.

They started to sell shrubs and fruit bushes and had a successful sideline providing window boxes for shops in town. However, Gerald was also doing deliveries for his father's laundry (and getting into trouble for mixing in plants with the clean linen!) while Rosemary became a busy mother of three children under five. David Keyworth has given us more details of the nursery's development. He was working at the Botanic Garden, but went along to help Gerald in the evenings, the time when most of the work was done. He describes the greenhouses.

And he got a friend to build this series of little sort of very low greenhouses made of old sash windows. A real Heath Robinson … all held together by scaffold poles and what have you, but it was a start … We were doing absolutely everything. Yeah. Potting up, going out [delivering]. We used to do the hanging baskets for Joshua Taylor …

Gerald knew all the colleges because he took all the laundry around the colleges. So he knew, and his father knew sort of everybody. So it was a very close knit community and work was beginning to expand. The Arbury Estate was in the process of being built – a huge amount of work out there. And then as we got sort of bigger and bigger and took on a couple of blokes, got more and more sort of contracts, we started thinking we need bigger, bigger premises, you know.

They were approached by the entrepreneurial florist and greengrocer Peter Biggs about buying a nursery in Shelford Road and turning it into a garden centre, a new idea at the time, so Peter and Gerald and their wives became the owners of a 14-acre site, but only for a short time, because around 1968 they sold all but a few shares to David Rayner, who now owns the whole highly successful business. For a while chickens and goats were kept on the Ainger site, but it was no longer run as a nursery.

Scotsdale Laundry

The Scotsdale hand laundry (no. 301) next to the nursery had been run by three spinster ladies who used Tredgett's glasshouses as washhouses. It was bought by Dudley Turvill as a business for his younger brother, Ronald, to manage when he was demobilised from the Commandos in 1946. Ronald's daughter, Avril Dring, still lives in the neighbourhood and provided us with information. The laundry flourished as more work came in, turnover went up and in 1951 the business was amalgamated with the Swiss Laundry in Cherry Hinton Road. The two sites continued and the Scotsdale Laundry was automated and extended and took on the dry-cleaning operation. However, it was eventually moved onto the site of the Swiss Laundry in 1981. The laundry building was converted to a furniture showroom for John's, a firm in Bridge Street. Squash courts were erected next door by Ronald's brother Keith and opened in 1979, becoming extremely popular. However, after he died the valuable building land around it was eventually capitalised on. Avril concludes:

> 2013. Land adjacent to the site was purchased and the whole site marketed for redevelopment in a scheme for 27 residential units.

Finally, the site was sold to Laragh Homes, and Ainger Cottage, after being derelict for years and gutted by fire, was demolished in May 2020.

297-99 Histon Road when it was used as John's furniture showroom.

Clive Vale Nursery

Opposite Roseford Road was Clive Vale Nursery, started by William Dear in the 1890s and run by three generations of his family. William had three sons. The eldest, Percy, an air mechanic, died aged 22 in World War I and is buried in the family grave in Histon Road Cemetery. After William's death the second son, Horace, took on the business with help from his brother James, and then it passed to Horace's son Michael and his wife Gill. Next door to the nursery were two cottages built in 1866, now considerably altered. Robin Barrett, who lived opposite at 'West Gate' (now no. 316) Histon Road, with his grandparents next door at 'Altona' (now no. 314) says there was a passage on the left-hand side of the cottages to two large greenhouses where tomatoes, lettuces and cucumbers were grown. The nursery specialised in cut flowers, and on the left was a shed where bouquets and wreaths were made up. At Christmas, Robin helped to make holly wreaths with his friend Michael Dear who later inherited the business. All the produce was sold in Cambridge market, on the stall on the corner behind Great St Mary's, as well as at the nursery. H. G. Stanford went into partnership with Michael and was in charge of the site, and the other nurseryman, D. L. Marshall, used to drive his lorry up to Covent Garden Market early in the morning and come back loaded with fresh flowers for sale. They lived in the adjacent cottages.

Pat Parker, now living on the McManus Estate, remembers when he started to work with Michael Dear.

Well, it was just general nursery work like cutting flowers and weeding. But as I got on and I learnt to drive, I then used to take the van down to the market square, unload it, and then do the same in the evening. And during that time, if there was any wreaths to be delivered to the funeral people I'd deliver them …

He describes the varieties of flowers.

Yeah, there was sweet peas, dahlias, chrysanths, alstroemeria, stocks … That was basically the basis of the nursery, with just the chrysanthemum and the dahlias … for a time we used to grow our own. They used to purchase daffs and tulips, he'd go up to Spalding to get them. But as time

Michael Dear and his assistant, Violet Tolliday.

went on, they found it easier to buy them in and then sell them on rather than having all the trouble of growing them.

The end of the nursery came suddenly, when Michael Dear died in 1977 at the early age of 42. Pat has a story about it.

Not long before he died he was talking in what we call the flower shed with little Elsie Chapman. And he told her that the back door knocked and he went out of the door and he thought it was strange because that was all enclosed in because of the dog and there was nobody there. And he was telling Elsie Chapman this and she suggested that 'somebody from the other side wanted you'. And not long after that, that happened a couple of times, three times, I think not long after that … he went.

Mrs Parker thought she saw him once.

I could have sworn he was standing in the room beside us.

MAP 2

Residents in Roseford Road 1939

THEOBALD 67 66
SHEPHERD 65
BENNETT 64
JOSLIN 63
CANNELL 62
THOMPSON 61
PARKINSON 60
PAPWORTH 59
ELDERKIN 58
BOSWORTH 57
MOORE 56
NEWMAN 55
BAILEY 54
BICHENO. 53
Dr GEE 52
MILLS 51
HOBSON 50
PARKER 49
NEAME 48
SALISBURY 47
SWORD 46
45
TAYLOR 44
ALLEN 43
WEBB 225' DEPTH
JAMES. 41
40

39 HILL
38 CHILT
37 FRANKL
36 DEAR
35 REEKIE
34 WITT
33 CHAPMAN
32 SHILLITOE
31 GARRETT
30
29 BROOM
28 MOORE
27 QUINTON
26 TOLLIDAY
25 FRENCH
24 CLARKE
23 WILKIN
22 BROWN
21 COE
20
19 PARSLEY
18
17 CHAPMAN
16 RICHARDS
15 ROBERTS. H.
14 ROBERTS. W.
13 HODGKINS.

NEW ROAD 30' FRONTAGE

BRANCH. N.
BUTLER
WILKIN ?R.
Watson
MALLETT
TOPPER B.
BUILDING LINE

Cooper
Bromwich
Barrett
Lochman
PROVIDENCE VILLA.

HISTON ROAD

Roseford Road

The cluster of houses fronting on to Histon Road at the junction with Roseford Road is described by Alec Forshaw in his book *Growing up in Cambridge*. His parents moved into the corner house (no. 320) in 1949. Two doors away, towards Histon, lived Alderman Howard Mallett who was Mayor of Cambridge in 1954 and was driven around in a black limousine.

It added a brief air of distinction to our little group of houses.

The land on which Roseford Road was built was sold off (by The Master, Fellows and Scholars of St Catharine's College), to a Mr Waterson, and divided into 68 plots that were offered for sale in 1929. They were a generous size with 30 foot frontages. On the north side, they were 225 feet in length and on the south somewhat longer, no doubt to allow for the drainage ditch that ran along the bottom of the gardens on that side. This is shown as a 'Public Drain' on old maps. Plots adjoining Histon Road had already been allocated and in some cases built on. Jackie Bartholomew (née Taylor) has supplied us with a lot of detailed information about the road.

The first house to be built in the new road was on plot 44. This house was built in 1930 for my father and mother, Ted and Ruth Taylor, and in March 1931 they moved in. My father had the opportunity to name the road but declined, and it was named by the landowner, Mr Waterson, after his niece Rose Fordham. Other houses were soon built and occupied mostly by young couples.

We had a big garden and had access to the fields beyond so had happy times with this freedom, especially at harvest time when we made little houses in the stooks of wheat. Our road was a cul-de-sac and there were few cars, so it was safe for children to play in the road.

Patricia Twinn (née Tolliday) has lived in Roseford Road nearly all her life. She remembered her parents telling her that the plots cost £80 each and the houses were bought off plan from a number of builders, with the clients able to specify their requirements.

My grandfather helped build these and several others down the road, but a lot of them were done by Mr Bicheno. Now my parents, when they had

Roseford Road plan with names of residents in 1939.

this house built, they would have liked a double bay at the top but it was to be a bit too expensive; they couldn't manage it.

Mr Harry Bicheno, an Australian, bought several plots for his family. He had his own house built (then no. 53). His granddaughter Dorothy writes:

He might have had 54 and 66 built too as these were my father's sisters.

Mr Taylor recorded that these were built by Jackson's of Hauxton.

Originally, the road was in Chesterton, then the boundary changed so that it was part of Impington and then Cambridge County Council took it over. In the decade before the war, the unmade sand and gravel road surface was tarmacked, the gas lamps, tended by a man with a bicycle and a ladder who came to light them, gave way to electric street lighting. House owners had to pay to be connected to a sewer, replacing the cesspits half way down the gardens, which were liable to overflow.

Conditions in the first houses strike us now as rather primitive. Patricia Twinn continued:

We had an outside lavatory which was round the back: in the winter had a candle in it, had no electric. I used to go out the back door, and the wind – 'cos the trees used to go 'whoo' – I used to go back against the wall round, scuttle in the loo with me matches and light the candle [laughs].

It was cold, it was cold, but didn't have central heating. Used to put our clothes in the bed in the morning; when you got up, and inside of the windows was just frosty; you could run it down, and there was just frost.

And we had an old electric fire, which you plugged in to the centre, which would be deadly today wouldn't it [horrified gasp]? And your iron was plugged into the plug at the top [laughs].

Downstairs they had a coal fire in a grate and a coal stove in the kitchen with an oven at the side, which her mother used to polish with black lead. Hot water in the bathroom came from a brass geyser.

It was huge, stood about three-foot high, and you had to light it with a match, and it went 'bang' [gasps], and then it lit up, and – you know – it heated the water, and that's how you did it.

Roseford Road in 2020.

After one disastrous Christmas when the pipes froze while they were away, and water came through the ceiling, the family shut up the bathroom in the winter.

There was no lavatory up there, you see, and what we used to do, we had a bath in the kitchen here … a tin bath in front of this little fire, and you were bathed in there, and the draught from the back door, I can't tell you! All you had round was your clothes horse with your towels hung on it to keep the draught off … It was a happy house, but as I say not so modern as most of the others which were built later across the road.

In the early days of Roseford Road there were a lot of young families moving in, leading to a feeling of community spirit that continued throughout the war years. Jackie Bartholomew has photos of children's birthday parties and the Guides. She is still in touch with Janet Hobson (no. 50) who emigrated to Canada.

Janet had a very large dolls' house which we could just fit into.

Her best friend was Avril Dring (née Turvill) who lived in the Scotsdale Laundry house; they used to ride to school on their bikes. She also mentions the Salisburys (no. 47), Betty and Sheila Orange and Rosie Sword (Ainger Place). One of her neighbours, Phyllis James (no. 41), became the famous detective writer P. D. James, later Baroness James OBE. Jackie writes:

Her brother had an aviary of budgerigars, and on a visit to see them my brother let out some of the birds and locked me in instead. Later in life Phyllis wrote to me and said how she enjoyed the fields behind their house and picking greengages in the orchard for Chivers jam factory. We also shared an interest in the school we both went to [Cambridge High School for Girls] and Phyllis said she [named] … characters in her books after some of the teachers there.

Patricia Twinn also remembers having good friends in the road to play with and plenty of ways to amuse them.

Well we just played out in the road, because it was a closed-in road, safe you see – you know it was quite a safe road – or in our gardens. We had, it's still there now, one of the sheds. We called it the dolls' house. Our mum cleared one shed, and we had a table and some chairs, and we played there, you know. Used to come in and have tea or bring it out there.

By the end of the war there were at least 40 children in the road.

The Arbury Estate

Alec Forshaw describes the Roseford Road area as a 'little hamlet' because it was separate from both Cambridge and Histon, surrounded by allotments, and to the north by extensive orchards of apples and pears belonging to Chivers. However, by the mid '50s the residents were anxious about the Council's plans for the Arbury Estate, which 'cast a great shadow over the neighbourhood'. In 1953 Arbury smallholders were given notice that their land was required for building and two years later the development plan was revealed. This was for the area to the south of Arbury Road. The plan was to accommodate 1,600 families in houses and flats, some of them built by developers. Facilities would include a shopping centre, a new primary school, two churches, a cinema (never built) and a public house.

Kingsway Flats, Carlton Way. Below: Arbury Court.

In 1957 construction began with the main access roads, then clearance of the ground, as vividly described by Forshaw.

> That autumn the field at the end of Roseford Road remained unploughed after the harvest, and weeds soon sprouted through the stubble. Before long, bulldozers and earth scrapers had moved in, grotesque machines which looked like giant grasshoppers. Hedges and trees were grubbed up into great mounds to be burnt in huge bonfires, the air was thick with the smell of diesel and exhaust fumes … soon lengths of string were pegged out in straight lines on the bare ground, marking the plots for new houses.

The flats in Carlton Way were finished in 1959. Eventually 20,000 new residents were housed on the estate, mostly from London but also from slum clearance in Cambridge. The memories of many of the first residents were of living on a building site with few paths and a great deal of mud. In the book *Arbury is Where we Live*, Mrs Walker recalls moving into Hawkins Road in 1963.

> Everywhere was dug up. There was a hole in the back garden, a massive hole which we asked the Council to fill in … everything was a shocking quagmire … There used to be planks up to the front door and I used to push the pram up to the front door because you see everyone was desperate to get into the houses.

It was quite a long trek to the shops.

> We used to have to shop either at the Co-op down on Milton Road or at Arbury Court – there was one or two open there; but of course not all of them.

The number of shops grew as the population increased. Eventually Budgens moved across from Histon Road where it had been in competition with the Co-op.

Rosemarie Hutchinson, who grew up on Histon Road but then lived in the north of England, moved back to Arbury when she got married.

> Yeah. The maisonette on the Arbury at Cockrell Road … we lived on the top floor. We got the sun in the winter, you know. Yes, quite nice

neighbours … The lady next door, we used to talk together, hanging out washing … And then there's another family further down. She was a cook. What was it – oh it's Jo. Yeah, Jo. They were black. We got on very well with them. Delicious smells coming from that kitchen.

The part of the Arbury Estate that fronts onto Histon Road was built after the Roseford Close prefabs had been demolished. In Hazelwood Close the handy local store, opened in 1990, is now also a Post Office, and is run by Nick Patel.

Further development to the north

With the rapid development of Cambridge, and the steeply rising price of land, it was perhaps inevitable that there would be further building along Histon Road. The fields and some of the allotments were replaced by the small-scale developments of Brownlow Road, Blanford Walk, Blackwell Road and Brierley Walk in the 1960s, and Chancellors Walk, built in the 1990s on the former Clive Vale Nursery land. The houses in these modern developments are all on small plots.

Clive Bowring moved into Brierley Walk in 1966.

We moved in when it was – just before it was finished and the developer was still on site constructing houses in Brownlow Road, having developed Blackwell Road first and Brierley Walk first.

The BEN development corporation would have bought the land from the Fellows and Master of St Catharine's College who were the then owners and they probably bought the land around about 1960/61 from the previous owner, which was Chivers Farms, who were farming a lot of land in this particular part of Histon Road.

Clive came to work at NIAB on the Huntingdon Road, choosing to live just across the fields.

Yes, there was a right of way across from Histon Road to Huntingdon Road. And … it was all concrete and tarmac most of the way. And there was a very pleasant, pleasant way to start the day by going through the old apple orchards.

The orchards were owned by Chivers and the land on the far side belonged to NIAB.

And they had owned that piece of land since 1919 when the National Institute of Agricultural Botany was constructed. And those were the first fields that they used for trialling and testing seeds and varieties of agricultural and horticultural crops … I should say that the land has recently been bought by the developers and they're currently building on this. This is part of Darwin Green, of course.

Clive speaks of the 'tremendous changes around here in the last few years', the building of the small roads off Histon Road, north of the McManus Estate, mentioned above; the imminent development of the squash court area and behind all these the vast swathe of land across to Huntingdon Road, already cleared, which could eventually accommodate 3,000 homes. Outline planning consent was granted for the first 1,593 units in 2013, plus a library, health centre and community rooms, a supermarket and a primary school. There will be an entrance on Histon Road nearly opposite King's Hedges Road.

Some houses in Brierley Walk border Histon Road, and so are affected by the plan to maximise the width of the road by cutting back vegetation, including an ancient hedge, in order to accommodate the footpaths, cycleways and a bus lane.

Allotments

Across the road, from Hazelwood Close on the edge of the Arbury Estate to the King's Hedges junction, run the allotments, all that is left of the very much larger site. Norma Davies remembered how much she enjoyed spending time on her allotment in the early '60s.

And then we had an allotment on Histon road. So I used to push the pram up through the little prefabs … Well, the allotment was the children … we spent all the days up there and we grew raspberries and vegetables, all sorts of vegetables, and we had plum trees up there. But they enjoyed pulling the water out because you had to pull a handle and get the water to water the plants. But it was fun. And they were always brown because it was so lovely.

The present Chairman, David Lawrence, joined the Chesterton Allotment Society in 1995 soon after he retired. It was formed in 1911 and was one of the largest in Cambridge, about 275 acres, although part of that was Hall Farm. He had been searching for an area called the Blackamoor Allotments, but he couldn't find out where they started until he came to one of our meetings.

We went right back to the 1900s because they must have been there because they were kicked off. But I mentioned it at the last meeting and a lady said, 'oh I know where they were'. In 1860, there was a lay out behind the Blackamoor's Arms, which is the pub in Victoria Road [now the Meghna Indian restaurant] at the back of Clare Street … There was a block of allotments. So we now know where it actually came from, but Cambridge City Football ground, Chesterton School, Bateson Road, Akeman Street and Windsor Road were the first developments on our allotment land and we slowly moved out. And that's how we've come on or gone down … There's still some allotments down Bateson Road, at the back of the green.

The allotments now cover 12 1/2 acres, holding about 400 5-pole plots. A pole is 5.5 yards square. Since becoming chairman, David has started an annual dinner and a best plot competition. He also likes to encourage children, organising visits for Mayfield Primary School, and turning a blind eye to grassed over play areas and toys on some plots.

Council houses with social housing, we all had your house and your back garden. But now a lot of them are in flats, they haven't got a garden.

He highlights two big changes affecting allotments in recent years: global warming and the diversity of the people cultivating the plots. He contrasts the appearance of his plot in May:

Lovely lush green and everything dug and ready – that was asparagus pushing through, the broad beans were going lovely.

with early September:

Allotment owners and their produce. Below: An old pump at the allotments.

Quite frankly, nine tenths of the allotment was dead. It was over, finished. Sun was so hot, but got me crop.

A few years ago, you didn't really need a hat on when you were down at the allotment, did you? It was completely different.

Sadly, the pond on the allotments has completely dried up because of new drainage patterns for Darwin Green. They used to have tadpoles, frogs and newts.

David emphasises how sociable the Allotment Society is, attracting many nationalities.

There are two Italians. Allotment life is completely different to outside. I have Wang, who is Chinese, number one. She's got the plot. Just comes in. Can't speak any English. We spend our time laughing to each other.

The Italians have grape vines and Wang grows peanuts. Another lady is Russian, an advocate of 'no dig' gardening.

And she's got chickens and she gets good crops … You go through the gate and it's a completely different world.

Here a remnant of the idyllic farming and growing community still clings on, albeit with some differences and surrounded by busy roads. We hope it will be retained for the benefit of local people.

World War II

Servicemen

As early as April 1939, young unmarried men aged 20–21 were called up. After the outbreak of war in September, conscription was extended to men aged 18–41. In 1942, the age was raised to 51, and unmarried women without children aged 20–30 were added. Some of the men in the Histon Road area could claim exemption as essential workers – farm labourers and employees of Chivers Factory, for example. During the war, Chivers supplied 40,000 tons of food to the armed forces. But in many homes, mothers were left in charge as their men went off to war.

During the war, anxious families waited for news of loved ones who were scattered all over the world. Ann Whitmore remembers a worrying time.

My oldest brother, John, was in the war, and my cousin, they were both in the Navy. My mum, they were always listening to the news to find out what was happening. And I can remember my mother getting terribly upset because she hadn't heard from my brother … I found a letter the other day … that my sister actually wrote to the naval officer to find out information of what had happened to John. But fortunately, all was well; the ship had been bombed, had been struck, but he was safe and he was in Calcutta, in India.

Patricia Twinn's father, a commercial traveller, was in the Home Guard.

Then in 1941 he was called up, and he was in Burma four years. We didn't see him for four years. Nah, he was just a village boy from Histon and he went to Burma as a driver/mechanic of a tank. I mean that was wonderful, isn't that wonderful for the education? … Yes, he kept in touch as best he could, but it was a worry. Could go weeks and weeks and then you'd have five letters come at once. My mother wrote every day to him and that you know, and it was lovely, really.

Of course, our interviewees were too young then to serve, but David Lawrence remembers being called up after the war and he showed us a picture of himself in uniform.

Ted Taylor with his stirrup pump.

I did my national service in the Royal Marines, and that first photograph is taken with me sitting there, that portrait. I was 18 and four months, round about, because I had to do three months' intensive training before they'd allow you out of the barracks.

His older brothers were in different services.

It was after the war, but servicemen were required and it was quite a good life. Robert went into the Royal Marines and Bernard went into Fleet Air Arm.

War damage

Compared with some cities, Cambridge was not badly damaged by bombing, but 51 houses were destroyed and over 1,000 damaged, especially near the station, where Vicarage Terrace suffered one of the earliest hits. In January 1941, a Dornier aircraft bombed the Mill Road bridge in another attempt to disrupt rail travel, including movement of essential supplies. About 30 people were killed during the war. Residents were very conscious of air traffic, both English and German. Barbara Jago concludes:

But we were lucky really in Cambridge we didn't have a lot of problems – we used to get the air raids quite a lot … with all the airfields in East Anglia.

Active preparations for defence started in 1938; sandbags were filled and trenches dug in Cambridge. Gas masks for the Castle ward were issued at Richmond Road School. Robin Barrett remembers that there was a concrete gun emplacement more or less opposite Carisbrooke Road, set up by the Army in case invading Germans approached Cambridge from the direction of Milton. The expectation was that the enemy tanks would use Histon Road as their route to Castle Hill, from where they could control the city. Residents on the eastern side of Histon Road down to Roseford Road were warned that, should this happen, their houses would be flattened to allow a clear path for firing across the fields. It was a terrifying prospect.

The Air Raid Precautions Department (ARP) from its headquarters at the cemetery organised a network of fire wardens that extended up Histon Road and across to Arbury Road. There was an ARP hut at the junction of

Histon Road and Roseford Road, and Jackie Bartholomew's father was one of eight air raid wardens in Roseford Road who took turns at watches during the night and recorded the sirens that warned of danger. They had little or no sleep one week in four when on duty. They also had to make sure that the blackout was observed. Householders were responsible for shutting out every chink of light, some even resorting to dipping their curtains in creosote. It could be difficult to see your way, says Ann Whitmore.

There were no lights and no lights in the houses. You can imagine Histon Road being pitch black.

Jackie continues:

During the war years, despite the unwelcome sirens signalling enemy aircraft around, we were fortunate to witness little bombing. My father's diary of 1940/42 records some bombs being dropped in Cambridge, the nearest being in fields near Arbury Road. Father was an air raid warden and spent many hours of duty in a little concrete building close to Histon Road.

A newspaper article shows her father, Ted Taylor, years later with the stirrup pump he was issued with. The wardens had a weekly meeting at the tennis court belonging to the Barrett family (now 316 Histon Road) to

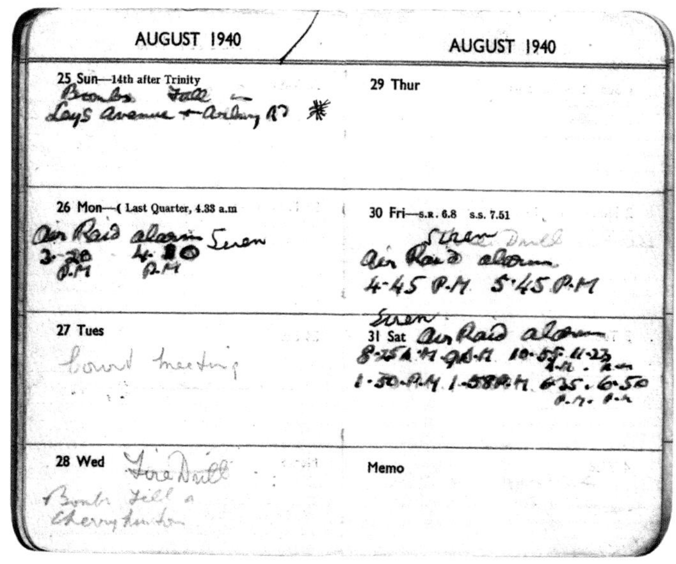

AUGUST 1940

25 Sun—14th after Trinity
Bombs fall Leys avenue + Arbury Rd

26 Mon—(Last Quarter, 4.33 a.m
Air Raid alarm Siren 3-20 P.M 4.20 P.M

27 Tues

28 Wed Fire Drill

AUGUST 1940

29 Thur

30 Fri—S.R. 6.8 S.S. 7.51
Air Raid alarm 4-45 P.M 5-45 P.M

31 Sat Siren Air Raid alarm

Memo

Ted Taylor's diary recording air raid warnings and bombing.

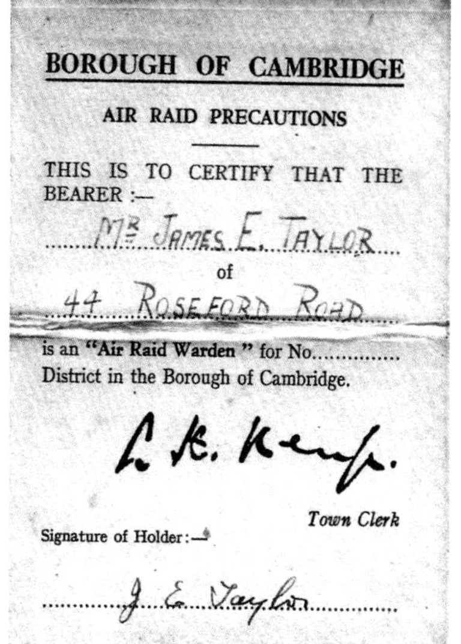

BOROUGH OF CAMBRIDGE

AIR RAID PRECAUTIONS

THIS IS TO CERTIFY THAT THE BEARER :—

MR JAMES E. TAYLOR

of

44 ROSEFORD ROAD

is an "Air Raid Warden" for No.............. District in the Borough of Cambridge.

Town Clerk

Signature of Holder:—

J. E. Taylor

Air raid warden certificate.

practise using the pumps. Mr Barrett was a warden and young Robin had to fill the buckets of water.

His diary records that high-explosive incendiary bombs fell in the vicinity of Huntingdon Road and Hertford Street between 11.25 and 11.40 pm on 28 September 1941. The local news reported extensive damage to telephone wires and public service pipes. We know that one bomb landed on the doorstep of 10 Huntingdon Road, home of Anna Crutchley's parents, but fortunately failed to explode. When Anna interviewed Ann Whitmore they were able to make a connection.

AC: It was at night, and Mum was in bed.
AW: Yes, it would make sense.
AC: Teaching herself the ukulele. So, she was sitting up in bed playing the ukulele. Dad was off, he was working in London at the time, at the Admiralty. And this bomb landed but didn't go off, on the doorstep … And you went round?
AW: Yes. And it could easily have been the next morning … But I remember going round to Huntingdon Road because they said that something had happened on the Huntingdon Road just at the top of Histon Road; it wasn't very far … And I remember seeing the damage that had been done to this house. I can't remember exactly. I suppose the windows had been blown, had they?

And I suppose there was a mess because they'd probably taken the bomb away. I don't know. It might even still have been there because I know there were bits all over the road. And this lady came down the steps with a bunch of flowers in her hand. And she said to me, 'Would you like to take these home to your mummy? Because', she said, 'I haven't got any vases any more and I have nowhere to put them'. And we think that must have been your mum … just amazing that, you know, after all these years.

On 12 February 1941 another wartime disaster was caused by an English Wellington bomber on its way back from a raid on the Continent crashing onto houses in Histon Road (no. 147 and Roseneath Villas) after the crew abandoned the plane. Three elderly ladies were killed and one injured. At the inquest, the crash was blamed on 'very bad weather', but it is more likely that the plane had been damaged by enemy fire. The crash happened only 100 yards from Ann Whitmore's home. She woke up in the dark to the sound of fire engines.

The lights were reflecting around the room. And I went downstairs and they said, 'don't worry, there's the plane crash down the road and your brothers have gone to see what's happening' … And sadly, there was a little shop with these two little ladies, kept this little grocery shop on Histon Road [no. 151]. And sadly, it had come down and taken the bedroom and the roof off that and the houses next door and landed on a tennis court. By the side of it. And my brothers next morning, well, sometime during the following week just sort of went and wandered all over it. And they actually cut a piece out of the side of the plane and they made a plate with it. They also cut the windows, which were sort of … Perspex stuff – I don't know what you call it … and made jewellery. They made rings and they made lockets that all the boys were doing, that all the kids around there were going and doing this sort of thing. And I've still got the plate. But yes, sadly, there were three people were killed in that … when that plane came down.

It was just sort of left. And there's this chest of drawers still in the bedroom … no roof or anything else. But I imagine that the old ladies' clothes were still inside those drawers. Because you didn't get any stealing or anything.

Around 1985, John and Gabrielle Sutcliffe bought half of the house that had been most damaged, without knowing the story of the crash. John said:

I could tell you, we first discovered when we were working on 153a, decorating the upstairs and I discovered the door architraves of the front bedroom had been punched into the floor – two inches I would say, and wondered why. A major trauma had happened to the top floor of that house … We were then told by a relation of a friend, or a friend of a relation about her father, who would have been a child in the area, in the '40s, that their house was hit by … [a plane].

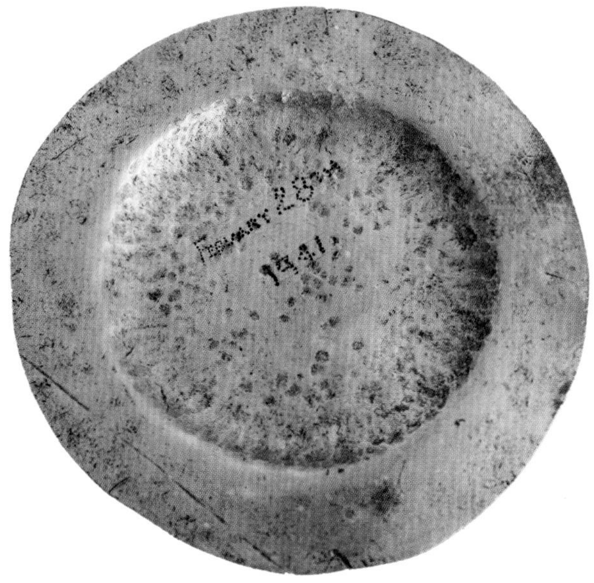

Plate made from crash material.

CAMBRIDGE DAILY NEWS, Thursday, February 13, 1941.

BOMBER'S NIGHT CRASH AT CAMBRIDGE

The wrecked houses in Histon Road caused on Tuesday night by the regrettable accident to an R.A.F. bomber which crashed on its way back from a raid on the Continent. Three old ladies were killed instantly.

Houses damaged by the plane crash. Below: The houses in 2020.

Air raid shelters

In the schools, the children were used to the drill for air raids. Ann Whitmore still remembers it.

The safety air raid precaution was we went into the porch of the – I don't know if it's even still there now, the porch of Richmond Road School. And we stood, sat there. And the one thing that they did do and when the sirens sounded, you go there, and I remember we had to say tables. We had to do our 10 times table. And we were always given the barley sugar.

Milton Road School had detached shelters according to Barbara Jago.

Somewhere around the back there was our air raid shelters and we all used to go running round there whenever there was an air raid. And if it went on for more than half an hour or something they used to give us an issue of Horlicks down there ... [chuckle] We were used to behaving because sweets were rationed in those days obviously ... we would hope it would last long enough to get a tablet of Horlicks.

David Lawrence was given five dolly mixtures at St Luke's School.

At home there were two types of shelter in use, Anderson shelters outdoors and Morrison shelters indoors. Barbara describes the latter.

Barbara: Had a metal top and ... so we had it as sort of a dining table and it was big enough to be the equivalent of a double bed size because two people could, two adults could sleep in it underneath. Then at the side there was mesh, wide mesh, erm – I can't remember how big it was now – but it was about a couple of inch square of wires – you know solid metal rather than just wires – you know they weren't flexible – that sort of hitched onto the side I think and I know that ... if our parents thought there was a danger of an air raid or, I don't know quite what criteria they used for this, but on certain nights I would be put to bed to sleep in there.
Interviewer: Was it comfy?
Barbara: Yes it was. There was a proper bed in it. I always liked it because I was allowed to have the dog in there with me.

Patricia Twinn describes the family's outdoor shelter in Roseford Road, which was not a success.

Oh yes, oh yes you had gas masks, and also you had to take an emergency ration, which was a tin and it had … biscuits or things like that, because if the siren went you had to go down to the shelter and that, you know, in the war, and my father built a shelter at the bottom of the garden and the siren went first time. 'Course my grandmother said it was church bells were for invasion, [air raid] siren, wail to start, clear note when it was all over. So my grandmother said 'no, gas, gas' she said, and got her gas mask on upside down. She got the birdcage in one hand, my father'd got the dog under his arm, and we rushed down to this shelter and my father wouldn't go in, my father wouldn't go in the shelter. My mother kept saying 'please come in, please come in'.

The next day we went down it filled with water. We suffer with water at the bottom of the garden, you see it's a flood plain down there, and that was just filled with water, so we never used it any more [laughs].

War work

As the war went on, women were encouraged or ordered to help in any way possible, and many from the Histon Road area worked part time for Pye's, the electrical firm, whose headquarters were in Chesterton. Two households in Roseford Road, the Salisburys and the Thompsons, turned their garages into workshops. Barbara Jago remembers her mother going there.

I think she just used to just go in the afternoons and it was all what they used to call 'wire twiddling' really for Pye's they were told … it was for aircraft and it was pretty basic things [probably circuit breakers] – they used to have the bundles of cut lengths of wire and they had to strip the plastic off … each end and just twiddle the ends of the wires together. That was basically a lot of what their work was and they had about er, five or six people and maybe more, I can't remember. But they had quite a big garage and they were turned into a sort of workshop because they had these little gadgets that were screwed on the tables where you put the wire in and it stripped off the plastic you know just that quarter of an inch off the end and they were fitted up to do this. And of course it got quite sort of party atmosphere in there – you know somebody would bake a cake and take it in for them you know when things were hard to come by in the way of rations and things. And I think they probably got a slight allowance for the owner to provide sort of tea and sugar for the people to get a cup of tea … while they were there. That was about it. And of course that was paid work – but that was part time but that was the only thing my mother ever did in the way of handiwork outside home.

Jackie Bartholomew remembers:

There were small offcuts from this [wiring] that we children threaded to make coloured bracelets.

Women might also be required to take in lodgers. Mrs Tolliday, on her own with two little girls, had to take in two workers.

Short Brothers had a factory over at Bourne there, you know … mending aircraft and that, and they came round and they put two men with, on, us, and my sister and I came down here [i.e. slept downstairs] … They billeted them on you; you had to. We had our beds here [downstairs]. Bill and Mr Dunn was his name, because he was an older man. They supplied, the government supplied, camp beds, pillows and blankets for them, which was for the beds; and also my mother was expected – I think perhaps a small payment was made, my mother was expected to feed them, do their washing, and pack … a box of food up, for them to take to work with them every day … she used to have to get up at six.

Children evacuated from London arrived in Cambridge early in the war and were housed with local families. Ann Whitmore remembered them at her school in Richmond Road.

And we did at that time [1942] have quite a few evacuees there. And we felt they were different, but we didn't really know the full story of it all. We didn't understand what was going on.

Other accounts suggest that evacuee families were sometimes treated with suspicion ('Londoners are nothing but trouble') and sometimes with kindness.

Italian prisoners of war helping to gather England's harvest in August 1941.

Food in wartime

Most gardens along Histon Road were large enough to grow fruit and vegetables and there were extensive allotments, so it was easy to follow the government's instructions to 'Dig for Victory' and to supplement the rations with chickens and rabbits. Patricia Twinn talked about wartime food.

I can remember sitting at the table and saying 'Mummy, I know now there's a war I won't have an egg for my breakfast every day' [laughs]. But you had chickens, you had a certain amount of meal given, you know … everyone had chickens, and rabbits 'cos we ate the rabbits and tame rabbits.

Mrs Tolliday was a good cook.

Rabbit pies my mother made. She used to stew the rabbit, take every bone out of it and then she would put carrot from the garden, and onions from the garden in with lovely delicate pieces of rabbit, put them into little pie dishes, and put pastry on top of it, you know, lovely pastry cook she was.

As well, you had a ration, and you had a book with points in it, which was for tinned fruit and that sort of thing, tins of peaches and that, which were quite rare. I can't say we were ever hungry.

I know we had a glut of plums in the garden. We had a big plum tree, and Chivers – do you remember Chivers? We had an old pram what the babies were in. They filled it with plums and we wheeled it – well we didn't 'cos we were young – wheeled it to Chivers for making the jam. You know you were allowed to make jam – you were allowed so much sugar.

Chivers employed Italian prisoners of war who lived in a camp at Histon. They were not regarded as a threat and were only lightly guarded. In fact people were quite friendly towards them, and in return they would make little wooden toys for local children. Barbara Jago says:

You used to see them walking up and down Histon Road and they had the sort of uniforms they had … a big circle of coloured – they were sort of like battle dress but on the back of the jackets there'd be this big circle of sort of yellow … so you knew who they were … And of course they were not sort of looked upon I don't think in quite the same way as the Germans.

Jackie Bartholomew remembered German prisoners still living along Histon Road after the war.

I used to admire their lunches of big chunks of bread and cheese.

No food was wasted. Ann Whitmore talked about the pigswill.

And I can remember Histon Road with the pig bins against the lampposts. You put all your garden food scraps and food waste, mostly vegetables and stuff in these bins and they were taken … I don't know where they actually took them to … farmers had them or who had them. But it was a national thing. And I can remember there being one just by the top of Canterbury Street.

The big treat for children was ice cream, which was delivered by a man on a bike. Patricia Twinn remembers it well.

Walls ice cream would come down in a van, in a tricycle with a box in front; and you had to put a 'W' in the window if you wished him to call. If not you went out, and he would open this lid, there was choc ices and blocks of those with little wafers that you put in. There was no cornets and soft ice cream in those days, it was purely little bricks, and there wasn't set ice cream, but mostly it was choc ices. Oh yes, and fruit lollies made of iced fruit. They were all in there …

Ann Whitmore's was sometimes homemade.

I remember my sister making ice cream in the garden. She always would make some ice cream. And I imagine what she'd done. She'd made a custard and she put it in … made a hole in the snow and she put the basin in the snow, and we all had ice cream … There was, there were some ice cream vans going around. It was Wall's ice cream, and they were the wafers, they weren't cornets … And you got them in paper. They gave me the biscuits. Then you unwrapped the paper of the ice cream and put them in a block.

After the war, imported food began to appear, including fruit she had never seen before.

These various products would come from other countries. And it happened that they were bringing in bananas and oranges. Well, they brought this banana in and I could not recognise it. And I said, 'What is it? What is it?' 'Oh, you have to peel it and you'll like it.'

The end of the war

Roseford Road celebrated the end of the war with a party for everyone in the street, as described by Jackie Bartholomew from no. 44.

On VE Day, which happened to be my ninth birthday, we danced around with lighted torches, tin cans on sticks, and had a big bonfire with an effigy of Hitler.

There was a much bigger party for VE/VJ Day later in the summer.

Dads built a bridge over the deep ditch at the end of the road, using tops from indoor [air raid] shelters. This led into a large field where a big marquee was erected. We children ran races, with prizes, and after a wonderful tea were given a book, a treat of ice cream and a new florin coin.

Trays of food came round and there was dancing to a wind-up gramophone.

Then we all gathered in the field for a memorable photograph.

This was one of several parties in the area in August and September 1945; others were held in Darwin Drive and Stretten Avenue, Gilbert Road, Garden Walk and Akeman Street.

Gradually the servicemen returned home and were welcomed. Ann Whitmore remembers:

I can remember when the end of the war and my brother came home from the war and we made – my aunt made this great big royal ensign because he was in the Navy and I can remember all the flags going all along the houses. And I was able to have a day off school because my brother was coming home and they did if you got a relation.

Patricia Twinn's father returned from Burma.

We were teenagers when he came back, and he said, 'I have some lovely dancing partners', and we used to go to tea dances with him. Didn't bother my mother …

He'd lost a lot of weight, 'cos he went down, you know, cut off for I think it was 12 weeks; well one of these big places out there. But, a very devoted couple they were, and my mother said she didn't resent, but she said when he came back, he locking the back door and winding up, you know, your alarm clocks on the mantelpiece in the kitchen, she thought 'I've been doing that for four years'. She was most thankful he came back.

They went away when my father came back, for a week on their own to Torquay.

Frank Holland of 68 Windsor Road returned in 1945 after an adventurous career in the RAF. He flew in one of the first operations on D-Day, then the next day had to bail out of his Hawker Typhoon at 500 feet, much too low for parachuting, but his fall was broken by landing in a tree. Fortune favoured him again when he was sheltered by French families and he eventually managed to rejoin his squadron. It must have been rather an anticlimax to come back to the family yeast business.

Sadly, many servicemen did not return. There are six buried in Histon Road Cemetery, one in a family grave and the others marked by Commonwealth War Graves Commission headstones (see Chapter 4). Other local men such as William Hayward of 214 Histon Road, James Haskins of 103 Stretten Avenue and Stanley Alfred King of 51 Akeman Street had no known grave. The first two died as they were being transported to Japanese POW camps in troop ships sunk by the Allies. Able Seaman Frederick Capon of Bermuda Terrace was lost in a storm in the Atlantic while defending a supply convoy.

A Commonwealth War Grave in Histon Road Cemetery.

741280 SERGEANT
W. E. LEVITT
PILOT
ROYAL AIR FORCE
13TH OCTOBER 1939 AGE 21

THE DEC
THE DEC
www.cambridge.gov.uk/chypps
01223 457873
J803 CEV

Growing up in Histon Road

Pre-war memories

The most enduring memories of our contributors were about their childhood. Some of these have already been recorded under other topics in the book, but there are so many that they deserve a chapter of their own. The recollections of our oldest contributors date to before the war, and we can go even further back with the written testimony of Ronald Pryor (1922–2011) supplied by his son Richard. He called it 'A Boy from Histon Road'. Ronald had a remarkable eye for detail, which is evident too in his paintings.

Young Ronald clearly had to amuse himself. Toys do not figure in his memories, but he was fascinated by everything going on around him.

> I was born and grew up on the very quiet road, corner of no. 10 Histon Road, which is just off the junction of Victoria Road where it joins Castle Street to Huntingdon Road. I used to stand on the doorstep of no. 10 and watch Tate & Lyle steam lorries I think they were Centinals [Sentinels]. Also sometimes on Mondays sheep were brought down Histon Road from the farms to the market up Hills Road, they went right through the town centre.

He watched other traffic in the road: Arnold the milkman with his horse and cart and the coalman next door.

> He would leave his horse and cart with its smell of fresh cut coal outside our house and of course he would put the horse's feeding bag on and the big old black and brown horse would shuffle this around and bang and scrape his hoof to attract Mr Smith's attention for a bucket of water.

It was heavy, dusty work for both man and animal.

From his front window Ronald could watch the men in the shop opposite who were cobblers, and he would go across to run errands for them or to see their animals.

> They used to have a large brown dog with whom I became great friends, they also had a large brown rabbit and one day as a small boy I went to see

The Mayfield Bus.

> the rabbit and in the cage were what appeared to be a lot of large potatoes. I went into the house and informed Mrs Corley, she laughed and said bless you my boy they are baby rabbits, they were the first young rabbits I had ever seen.

There is a feeling of very close neighbourliness and people looking out for one another, even though it was a poor area.

> At Bilton's Bakehouse, the bakery fence was one side of our garden, and often Joyce Bilton or one of her brothers, would call to my sister Joyce or myself Ron (Joyce) if one or both of us answered a bag would be thrown over with two freshly baked bread twists still hot from the oven. The smell from the bakehouse was wonderful.

It was common in those days for families to live close to one another and Ronald had relatives on his father's side a couple of streets away.

> My father's sister Joy living … nearby and popping in and out Benson Place just behind Histon Road off Cantaberry [Canterbury] Street where Grandfather Richard (Dick) and Grandmother lived (Sarah) with their eldest Shell shocked son Albert, and next door to them My father's Eldest Sister Ada with her second husband Ernie Joh(n)son.

From the relatives, Ronald overheard stories of the horrors of the last war and how his Aunt Ada's first husband had been killed in 1918. He watched badly disabled and gassed men in the area and knew children who had lost their fathers.

His grandfather, a 'fine hard worker' who had been a thatcher employed by Chivers in Histon, is brilliantly observed,

> Big heavy built-man, always wore a pair of calf length dark brown gaiters of thick leather, with two small brass buckles on the sides a thick watch chain across his waistcoat he never wore a collar on[ly] a tied patterned kerchief … on one occasion [he] showed us how he had found a nice bit of material to mend his Jacket lining. The bit of material was a Union Jack. I remember how bright it seemed and how my parents laughed.

Making do and mending was a standard way of life in this society.

Wartime

Sign showing the time of blackout.

From Ann Whitmore, Jackie Bartholomew and Patricia Twinn we have memories of growing up in World War II, also a time of economies and some hardship. Ann lived as part of a very large family at 75a Histon Road, and Patricia and Jackie in rather more affluent circumstances in Roseford Road. The children were not really scared by the situation, Jackie wrote.

Apart from the dreaded sirens, blackouts and food rationing we children were not too distressed in wartime although it was a great relief when the All Clear siren sounded as a few bombs and incendiaries were dropped not too far away.

Ann actually went to investigate incendiaries in Huntingdon Road and walked all round the plane that crashed in Histon Road. Patricia says they knew something big was happening when there was a lot of air traffic from Waterbeach, but her mother kept her anxiety to herself.

But then when you're 10 years old, part of it is an adventure. You know what I mean, you don't realise how awful it was, and I think now of my little mum, bless her heart, what they did, those mums; they all ought to have got a medal … they were absolutely wonderful.

American airmen were on the streets of Cambridge in the 1940s. Ann Whitmore encountered them when she went up the road to play outside Murkett's garage on the corner. The Yanks were known for being generous to children, distributing a novelty – chewing gum.

And I remember all these Americans coming up. We all used to say 'got any gum chum?' you know … And incidentally my sister was going out with an American and he would have food parcels and they would be interesting and he'd often give us things from that.

Her mum welcomed the American and Polish soldiers, saying 'I just hope that someone's looking after my son and I look after you'.

There were not a lot of holidays in wartime. Patricia Twinn used to go to relatives in Leiston, Suffolk, members of the French family of millers who owned the bakery in Searle Street.

They had a shop, a general store, and a big bungalow; but they got bombed and blown to pieces in the war. We thought it was a German, but they said it was an RAF plane that had brought its load back, and they were caught, and all of a sudden one went [off]. They said the tinned stuff was four streets away … Went and had a look at it. Well my: they were both killed. My aunt was blown to pieces, and my uncle got – they called it a blast. They said he hadn't got a mark on him. He was dead.

It was a traumatic event for a teenager to be caught up in. Being located near the Suffolk coast, Leiston airfield was often used by damaged planes returning from Europe and the little town was bombed more than once.

Children's games and other activities

This was still an era when children were left to their own devices and seldom supervised. Ann used to go to 'the Rec', which was then just an area of rough grass where she and her brothers could climb trees and play games like 'statues'. Without any adults around to restrain them, there were likely to be occasional accidents. In Ann's case she sustained an injury to her elbow that required several operations and altered her life, because it prevented her completing the 11+ exam which she would certainly have passed.

Another favourite playground for Ann was the cemetery, because her best friend Yvonne Pryor was the daughter of the keeper. The chapel in the centre was still there.

And we used to play mothers and fathers. And she'd be one side of the steps … there'd be steps going up to the chapel. And she'd be one side and I would be the other. And we'd have our dolls' prams and our dolls and we'd talk about those problems and our dolls.

They liked to play on the mound over the air raid shelter and there were some impromptu activities too.

Once, there was a cat killed on the road. And somebody put it in … they just put it inside the cemetery. And we felt so sorry, Yvonne and I, we went and got a spade and we dug and made a little grave for it and put some flowers on it. And … we found a little cross that nobody was using … and put it over the cat's grave.

With her brothers, Ann remembers going farther afield, presumably when she was a bit older.

Every day during the school summer holidays, the long summer holidays … we would be up, go to Newnham and we'd either be doing fishing for tadpoles or what have you along by Queens' College or else we'd be up at the paddling pool in the river.

Her dad drove a lorry for Chivers and it was her biggest treat to go with him to London, starting about 5am and stopping for a cup of tea at a transport café.

A Chivers' lorry in the '50s.

It was fantastic going out in the lorry so early in the morning because it was all up the old A10 and there would be the foxes right across the road and things that I'd never seen before … But dad then said, 'I'll show you where the king and queen live'. And I can remember him taking me down in the Chivers lorry, down the Mall to show me Buckingham Palace.

Roseford Road was a more isolated environment but it was a paradise for children, who could play in acres of surrounding fields and orchards. Alec Forshaw wrote:

I doubt that my parents ever really knew what we got up to.

Fruit picking at Cawcutts' Farm, a Chivers orchard.

Robin Barrett from Histon Road used to fly his kite in the field behind Ainger's Nursery.

Patricia Twinn seems to have stayed closer to home, playing with friends out in the street and in their sizeable gardens.

Well you didn't expect to be amused you know … you were encouraged to read. Milton Road Library was where you went … We always had books, plenty of books and that, and I love reading.

All the food was delivered, so they didn't often go to shops.

If we were going you went with your parents down town you know, but I know at Christmas my parents used to go down to Sainsbury's, which was along where Next is now [actually straight ahead if walking down Market Street to Sidney Street]. They had a big long Sainsbury's there, and [we] fetched the turkey.

She helped her father grow vegetables.

We had potatoes, runner beans over here, and you had carrots, onions, you know onion sets, you had it all down there, which you worked. And also we had blackcurrant and redcurrant bushes … You know you had good wholesome food.

The Twinns were more or less self-sufficient for fruit and vegetables, and this was a common feature of the area in the early to mid-20th century. Ronald Pryor reports that his father came home from a long day at Chivers to work on his 20-pole allotment. Barbara Jago has memories of fruit picking in the school holidays for cash.

Chivers had a lot of land down there and I remember picking strawberries and gooseberries … Well, we ate a few of course and then they used to be weighed and then you used to be paid and it wasn't very much of course but it was pocket money and when I was a bit older we used to go to Coton. Do you know that garden centre? … that was an orchard.

And there was picking apples and plums and of course having to go up ladders to do that and I was a bit older then because we used to cycle out there to do that. Yes, I suppose we cycled everywhere in those days.

Children's games do not change much over the years; women remember hopscotch and skipping ropes, hula-hoops and dressing up. In the '60s Jo-Anne Kocian played on the waste ground on the corner of Warwick Road before Belmore Close was built.

There was nothing there apart from a mound of earth and my friends and I used to slide down the mound on a tray.

They collected black slugs and kept them in a jam jar.

Marbles was the favourite and I remember once I lost one marble and a

Histon Road Recreation Ground in 2020.

little lad I used to be very friendly with, he found the marble for me, and he brought it round. We were in Chatsworth Avenue at the time … and he said 'I've found your marble Jo-Anne' and he blushed. He was so sweet – oh he was lovely.

Gangs of children

Older children often went around with gangs of local friends in the '60s. Terry Dunn was in a group of boys in Histon who loved trains.

One of the big things was trainspotting because at Histon they had, where the guided buses are now, they had steam trains going through and we were all mad keen on trainspotting and, you know, getting train numbers, all that sort of thing … we'd go up the line to Oakington or Swavesey, Longstanton, and get the numbers there, so it was always a big thing.

Later, on the McManus Estate, children stayed closer to home. Terry and Janet's sons were in an enterprising gang that once raised money from selling squash on the Green and regularly played tennis and cricket in the street. Janet Dunn recalls:

Wimbledon. His steps used to come out of the garage and one of them used to sit as umpire while they played tennis, but after Wimbledon that went away for another 12 months.

The Dunns held open house for children and so became very pally with their parents, many of whom still live on the estate.

Near the southern junction, on Huntingdon Road, Anna Crutchley and her older brothers joined with other children to play across the road in Byron House woods, attempting to shoot squirrels with bows and arrows, and they were joined by another group from Storey's Way. They were in and out of each other's houses all the time and the mothers were at home to keep an eye on them. None of this is possible for today's children, so it is looked on as a golden time of freedom.

Children also made friends at clubs such as Brownies at Mayfield, Guides at St Luke's, and Sunday school and the Crossways youth club at the Congregational Church, since demolished. Television was very new in the 1950s and few families would have had their own set. However, David Lawrence tells how he secured a few weeks of viewing.

I remember when we moved from Searle Street to Bateson Road because we had [a] fully electric house then and Pye did an airplane drop. They dropped a load of balloons with different tickets at the bottom. And if you found one of these, you could have a television for what, two months or something like that, for nothing. And I found one of these. So I gave it to mum and dad … first time we had a black and white set; there it was in one corner of the room with … a room full of people sitting right round the side – all the children sitting on the floor at the front. We had our own little cinema for two months.

School

Before Mayfield Primary School opened in 1962, Histon Road was in the catchment area for Richmond Road School. Ann Whitmore describes it.

Richmond Road School.

I suppose my first memories were going to Richmond Road School when I must have been five and all the memories that are connected to Richmond Road School during the war time, because this would be 1942 … And I could name quite a few of the children that were there.

It always seemed very cold in those days in the wintertime. I can remember the milk coming in and we had roaring fires in Richmond Road School. And we at least put the milk in, and we used to watch the milk and it would always be iced up. We'd always watch the milk pop up the top. And then it always had this horrible smell of stale milk in the room because of the way it bubbled over into the fireplace.

Richmond Road School was closed in 1962 and the pupils sent to Mayfield along with many who were moved from Arbury School. Jo-Anne Kocian says that her fondest memories are of Mayfield Primary School and the activities they had there. She describes the building.

It wasn't long after it opened that I went to Mayfield in the infants … I can remember when I started initially in the infants it was the ground floor classroom to start with on my first day. Then they started expanding the school and they brought in prefabricated classrooms. So then when I got to top infants we moved into the prefab classroom, which was lovely; it was lovely and warm.

PE in the big hall and we would have assembly in the small hall which also doubled as the dining room … my favourite lesson was writing. I learnt my handwriting then – and that was my favourite: I loved it … I remember the caretaker was Mr Lusher. I remember him and his family.

Mr Lusher's daughter Meryl recalled her father working all summer clearing up after the builders and removing the remains of old pig pens left on the former allotments before the school opened. Jo-Anne continues:

Milton Road School.

I also went to Mayfield as a Brownie so … all the usual Brownie activities – games and we prepared for our badges, did first aid courses, yeah it was lovely and the Brown Owl was Mrs Willis.

She mentions that the school had a swimming pool, on the right behind the bungalow, which opened for the summer holiday club.

Mayfield has expanded a lot since then. The school burnt down in a disastrous fire in 2004 and was closed for nearly three years, but that gave an opportunity to involve teachers and children in a redesign. The landscaping encouraged outdoor learning, which has become a feature of the school. The playground double-decker bus is an unusual acquisition, paid for by the PTA and decked out with an Alice in Wonderland theme in 2014.

Our older interviewees progressed from Richmond Road to Milton Road School, quite a long walk from Histon Road. It was then in a Victorian style building on the corner of Gilbert Road, opened in 1908. Patricia Twinn was enthusiastic about it.

It was a big red-brick school. I've got a brick out there from it [laughs], but it was, it was an excellent school, excellent school. A Miss Shry was the headmistress, and Mr Varley was the headmaster of the school … my mother was a very clever lady, and she won the Hobson scholarship for East Anglia to the County School and her name was on a board, up in the hall. (This was Violet Tolliday, photo. p. 77.)

Patricia thinks she and her sister cycled home to Roseford Road for lunch; there were no school dinners.

Some children caught the bus with a relative and were dropped off. As traffic increased, a lollipop lady was employed to take them safely across the road. Ann Whitmore had to walk and was frightened to make her way home during the blackout.

And I used to have the torch. And I used to walk along the middle of the road because I felt safer in the middle of the road because there was no cars. And that is hard to believe today, isn't it? No traffic.

Thinking about school, she remembered that there were only two male teachers because all the other men were doing war service. She also came up with a funny anecdote.

I can remember this chocolate powder coming from Canada to be given to all the children … we had to take a container … and we'd never had anything like it because you couldn't get sweets or anything. Not very easily. And I can remember going down at the desk and taking mouthfuls of this chocolate powder, which I thought was wonderful. And my teacher called out, 'Ann Free, what are you doing? Put down your desk. I hope you're not under your desk. I hope you're not eating that chocolate powder.' And I came up with my face full of chocolate. 'But no, Miss Tredgett, no!' And that was that.

Several people remarked that discipline was good in the schools. Children were mostly well behaved. Barbara Jago says:

I don't remember many instances of people answering back or being cheeky or difficult.

However, on her last day at school, Maureen Newman recalls crossing Jesus Lock and throwing her beret into the weir in celebration. She said that the wind had blown it off!

Our interviewees went to quite a variety of secondary schools; Chesterton, which was then segregated into boys and girls, the County Boys School and County Girls School, the Perse Boys, and St Mary's Convent, which was then free. Some continued to the Regional College for vocational training or to the Tech for School Certificate and a few went on to university. It was not uncommon to leave school at 16 and go to work. Chivers were the biggest employers and there were also jobs in Addenbrooke's Hospital, Cambridge University Press, small local factories such as Gray's and shops and offices. David Lawrence was quite unusual in commuting to London for a job with British Rail, leaving on the 7.02 to Liverpool Street every day. Commuting was the shape of things to come in Cambridge.

Holidays

The people of Histon Road seemed very happy to spend their holidays by the nearest coastline, in Norfolk and Suffolk. They went to self-catering accommodation, sometimes places owned by relatives. Patricia Twinn remembers that in 1939 her family went to Kessingland near Lowestoft.

It was a camp site, and we had what had been old railway carriages, and they were made into, you know, bungalows and things; and I know it had a tennis court. My parents played tennis and that, and then there was a stream that went around, and we could swim in that; and the dog went with us.

Patricia and her husband Derek still went there in the '50s, taking their children to stay in a bungalow like a prefab and meeting up with parents and grandparents.

They [her parents] came down for the day, and my grandmother and Derek's mother came on the coach. But families kept together, didn't they, but they don't so much, now.

Rosemarie Hutchinson's mother died when she was eight and their next-door neighbour had also lost his wife, so the families combined for a holiday every year.

Well, we'd always go to Great Yarmouth in the holiday with Mr Harvey the butcher who lived next door, and his sister, because his wife died, and his daughter Eileen … stay in a caravan or two caravans. It was down the coast. And my auntie at Histon, she had a bungalow in the sand dunes, at Hemsby. So they'd come over to us for, like, sandwiches and cake and … or we'd go over there, you know, and have supper or something.

When Rosemarie's own children were small they went to the auntie's bungalow and now she takes her grandchildren to a caravan at Caister. Simple seaside holidays are very much a favourite of the older generation.

Teenagers

Teenagers were hanging around in groups as early as the '40s, as Patricia Twinn confirms. That is how she met her future husband.

There was groups, what they called gangs. They were groups of girls and boys, and they met mostly where the swings and roundabouts were on Jesus Green … and Derek and I kept together, which is a long time.

She was 16 and married at 21. This was not at all uncommon in the '40s and '50s. Ann Whitmore met her future husband at the Crossways Club, a youth group attached to St Luke's Church in Victoria Road.

And we were probably one of the last ones to get married because my girlfriends all married older men who had money and they went straight to new houses … Whereas John was still at college, having gone straight from the Perse School at 18 into the R.A.F. to do his national service for two years. And then he went to Goldsmith's College London for teacher training. He was in his last year at Goldsmith's, and we were both 21 and all our friends kept expecting us to announce our engagement.

After saving up for a wedding they eventually married in 1959 at St Luke's Church when Ann was 23. National Service ended the following year, although those who had deferred still had to do it.

The Dorothy Café in Hobson Street, described in the '30s as 'a mecca for ballroom dancing', was still going strong after the war and was a good place for young people to meet. Barbara Jago was a student nurse, working shifts, and said it was a popular place to go in her long morning break.

But they had a ballroom, lovely ballroom with a sprung floor up on the first floor. And in those days they used to have coffee dances in the morning and tea dances in the afternoon where you could go and just have a cup of coffee with tables around the room … and there was a dance. And that was the same in the afternoon. And of course in those days there weren't many women around in Cambridge … only two women's colleges. And so nurses were quite in demand.

In the '60s teenagers were just coming into their own after the dull years of post-war austerity. Rosemarie Hutchinson left school at 16 and went to work in the knitting factory in Searle Street. Asked what she did in the evenings, she said:

Probably go to my friend Josephine and we'd play records. Mm. Put on nail varnish or just maybe watch telly. We'd go to the cinema on a Saturday … Yeah. Kids in the '60s … I remember going to see the Beatles when they were at the Regal. Saw the Bee Gees there.

The Regal in St Andrew's Street was the largest cinema in Cambridge, opened in 1937. Its upper floors are now the Arts Picturehouse.

Terry and Janet Dunn met in the '60s when they both worked as administrators in the NHS. They were happy to talk about their courtship, over 50 years ago.

Terry: I wasn't very confident at all, you know, and I plucked up courage to ask Janet out to a New Year's Eve dance at Stevenage for some friends of ours who were together, worked in the same office, and the idea was to go with them, in a foursome. And I asked Janet out, knowing full well that she would say no. Before I hardly got the words out, she said, yes!
Janet: I'd love to.
Terry: And so it all started really. And I proposed to Janet. Janet was only 17 at the time. Obviously, we had to get permission from her dad through all this. Because it was 21 – the age of consent. I asked him if I'd got his permission to marry his daughter. And he said, 'no way'. He said, 'you're both far too young' … but Janet's mother said, 'don't worry, I will talk him round'. So I asked him again at Christmas and he said yes. So we got engaged, actually 12 months after we met, and we married.

The Dunns spent their leisure time ten pin bowling and going to the cinema and enthusiastically embracing the movements of that era.

Terry: We had a Lambretta, a number [Series] 2 two seater, wasn't it? And I was always mad on my bikes and scooters. Oh yeah. We had mullets you know, [a hairstyle in which the hair is cut short at the front and sides but left long at the back]. We've been through it all actually.
Oh, actually Mods and Rockers and Ban the Bomb we were involved with as well. Oh yeah, Ban the Bomb, CND, and the summer of love and all that sort of thing. Flower festivals, you name it.

So the war babies and the baby boomers grew up and enjoyed a better standard of living, mortgages that allowed them to buy their own homes, and, crucially, a better education for their children. Many proud parents said their children had done well at school and gone on to university. Of course, the increased opportunities have led them to leave Cambridge for jobs all over the world, reducing the closeness of families who in the past would have lived in the same street or town.

Ann Whitmore remembers her wedding at St Luke's Church.
Someone hid confetti in her umbrella!

WELCOME TO
SAINT LUKE'S
CHURCH CENTRE
Please use the south door for
access to the church service

Afterword

The Histon Road scheme

Lilian Rundblad, leader of the oral history project.

The knowledge that Histon Road would inevitably soon change seemed to be a catalyst for seeking out and preserving memories of past lives. People were anxious to set things down while they could still remember them, before they were overwhelmed by new events.

The news that a major project was going to substantially affect Histon Road slowly filtered into our community from 2016 onwards. For most people it was another two years before they realised the scale of the proposals and the elements that would affect them personally. This was when a survey was organised by the Greater Cambridge Partnership mentioning a bus lane, floating bus stops, removal of parking bays and new landscaping. Some homeowners were threatened with the loss of trees and hedges from their frontages and part of their front gardens. Residents with no previous interest in local politics joined the Residents' Associations that were formed. Anna Crutchley said:

> We had started Benson Area Residents' Association … we all got together and everyone really enjoyed meeting each other … but interestingly, it was at the same time as the Histon Road project was coming up and ever since then we have all been involved with that, and … if we hadn't set up the Residents' Association, we wouldn't have been able to gather people's ideas and worries and concerns and communicate them through our weekly email updates and so on.

Histon Road streetscape.

Lilian Rundblad added:

I think the unity was the good thing that came out of all this from Histon Road, that the residents' associations got to know each other and work together ... And then of course after that FeCRA, the Federation for all the Cambridge Residents' Associations, expanded enormously.

Large numbers attended the public exhibitions and Local Liaison Forums (LLFs) organised by the Greater Cambridge Partnership to 'have their say'. We shouldn't deny that there was initially a great deal of anger in the community. Change brings fear and anxiety. Lilian Rundblad remembered the first LLF.

But ah, yes, I would say there was a war actually, during that meeting.

This eventually changed to a more collaborative approach. After lengthy consultations, some ideas put forward by local people have been incorporated, some decisions reluctantly accepted by them and others supported in the hope that they will produce the desired outcome. No one can object in principle to better public transport and safer cycling and walking: we wait to see if it is achieved.

The road and its traffic

One thing that is mentioned all the time is the amount of traffic on Histon Road and the difficulty of crossing. It is now described as a 'key gateway' to Cambridge. Anna says:

This is all about the rebuilding of Histon Road and Milton Road in response to the expansion of Cambridge. And the new villages that are going to be built to the north, and how to manage the transport of the people coming into Cambridge.

She pointed out:

Histon Road isn't bad during the daytime ... it's just at the rush hours that it piles up and is congested.

Clive Bowring, living at the north end of the road, said the same thing.

That's why we question very much whether it's going to help considerably, because we have never, ever, witnessed any holdups at this end of the road for buses or trucks or any cars or anything.

In reply, Alison Wilson said:

The hold up that I can foresee is at Carisbrooke Road because there's going to be a crossing there, just where the exit is from our estate [McManus]. Yes. And on the other side, is going to be another exit because of the new road and the squash court houses, as I call them – all together.

There has been much concern that a wider arterial road will separate friends and neighbours. This was one of the first things that struck Lilian Rundblad.

I thought … we have to keep the community together. Both sides of Histon Road have to be able to go across and talk to each other. And it's important for the schoolchildren because they go to different schools, even if they live on one side and the school is on the other side, and crossing Histon Road is important for everybody.

Alison Cox mentioned the waiting time for crossing at the traffic lights.

If I could change anything I would reinstate zebra crossings along Histon Road … rather than light-controlled crossings.

As a cyclist, she is also concerned about the road surface and visibility at night.

We've got a lot of potholes so you need to be able to see the surface of the road really well to make sure you're not going to go down a hole in the road … I as a cyclist often end up in the drains in the gutter and it's difficult when the weather's bad to cycle down there.

Karina Cleland added:

The pavements are horrible.

We certainly hope the provision for cyclists and pedestrians will be much improved by the project, with wider lanes and safer junctions. Nearly all parking has been removed from the road, a hugely controversial issue. Alison Cox believes that deliveries and illegal parking should also be tackled.

I would send somebody down there at regular intervals to make sure people don't park on the double yellow lines, particularly delivery vans. Any new buildings that are put in, especially businesses I think, should think very carefully about having adequate parking because if you are going to visit a shop unless you're young and fit and you're prepared to carry quite heavy loads you're going to be buying something and carrying it back. You do need to stop safely. There's a lot of elderly people in the local community who need to be able to stop [park] their cars safely. If I was redesigning buildings I'd make sure that all the shops, for example, had an area where they could take their big lorries, vans, delivery vehicles around the back with a dedicated area for them to unload and offload leaving Histon Road free for the buses to go along without being held up, for example at the petrol station.

Other people wonder if enough thought has been given to the elderly. Looking ahead, Alison Wilson says:

You wonder if you will be able to use your car at all in the future. We [older people] can't be cycling in 10 years' time. So I will be totally dependent on the bus. Buses at the moment are somewhat erratic. Every 20 minutes. So, we just hope that will improve.

Lilian Rundblad is afraid there won't be a safe route for mobility scooters, tricycles and box cycles.

Coming like me on my mobility scooter, and things like that, you need a little bit of space if you meet people coming the other way on the road. It is impossible in 1.1 metres. My scooter would just chuck them out in the road or in the cycle lane or something like that.

Jo-Anne Kocian thinks the bus system used to be better in the past.

It used to be good originally. We've always been served by a country service, Histon to Cottenham service that comes along Histon Road. And at that time there was the 139 bus that used to take us round what is now the Grafton Centre but of course it wasn't then. It used to go to New Square, Fitzroy Street onto East Road. That was very useful, as well as another bus service used to terminate in – oh where was it? … Drummer Street bus station. So that was very handy for the town as well.

There has been talk of eight buses an hour; the question is how many will stop for the residents of Histon Road and whether the station and Addenbrooke's Hospital can be reached without changing buses.

The green scene

Nothing has aroused more passion than the loss of trees and other vegetation in the area.

We need trees. It makes it a lovely road. It gives it character. And it will be a great, great loss to just make it into one of these straightforward [highways].

Karina Cleland speaks for most residents. A strong symbol of community protest has been the yellow ribbons tied on the trees under threat all the way along the road, but particularly noticeable on the row opposite Borrowdale. For some people passing through on their way to Histon and Cottenham it was the first they knew about the Histon Road proposals. The schoolchildren from Mayfield readily turned out to express their love of trees.

Histon Road Area Residents' Association passed a resolution:

The streetscape with trees articulates a sense of place and provides aesthetic interest, better air, better drainage, and lower flood risk. They have a considerable amenity value throughout the seasons.

Some house owners realised that they were going to lose trees and hedges from their front gardens, where they had crossed what the Council considered to be the boundary line; in particular Molly Sneddon defended her listed poplar.

Listed poplar tree, threatened with destruction.

Pollarding in progress: a compromise.

Speaking of her own neighbourhood, Norma Davies said:

It's taken the McManus Estate all these years to make it into something really good, and now they're taking the trees down … and I love hedges and trees because you see such a lot of wildlife.

Clive Bowring's house backs onto the road, bounded by a hedge. His research revealed that it was most probably an ancient boundary.

There was a very ancient hedge between the rear gardens of Riley Walk and Blanford Walk … That was probably built some time after the enclosures, because the Histon charity that bought the land in the 1840s would have required them to put a boundary around the land that they had bought, and this was in the days before barbed wire. [It's] mainly hawthorn, but some other species as well. And now we understand they're going to rip it out at the end of this year.

At this end of the road a three-metre high fence will be provided, suitable for climbing plants, and each owner can choose a mature tree to be planted on their land. We hope that this will be sufficient to shield them from passing buses. Residents have been very involved in choosing the landscaping of the junctions, where in most cases mature trees have been cut down, though others will be planted. There is a promise that there will be no reduction in the number of trees overall.

Many people have said how much they miss the rural walks across NIAB land to Huntingdon Road. Dog walker Barbara Jago mentioned that there is no longer anywhere suitable for dogs in the vicinity.

I used to use the car most days to take him somewhere off the lead because you know, he can't [run free] round here and now that the NIAB ground up the road has largely disappeared. You know, that was the nearest place where I could take a dog for a walk.

But eventually there will be some compensation as Lilian explained.

Darwin Green now is building a country park and leaving little lakes because they couldn't fix it properly for the construction of houses. They have stopped everything from A14 and down to King's Hedges and in there will be a country park, which is a good idea. I mean it would be lovely to have somewhere to go. We would have loved to have a park to take the kids to when they were small, you know.

In summer 2020, having done what they can to influence the project for the better, residents simply have to wait and see how it will turn out, putting up with much inconvenience as the road is closed in one direction over a total of 18 months or more. There is an atmosphere of resignation, exemplified by Terry and Janet Dunn.

Terry: But that's progress, I suppose …
June: Yeah. Change the character.

And, of course, as well as bringing people together to debate decisions, the Histon Road project has led to our oral history recordings, photographs, exhibitions and this book celebrating the past.

Darwin Green wild flowers. Below: Darwin Green prepared for building by developers.

The beginning of the roadworks, February 2020.

PRINCE HENRY COURT
DAIRY TAKES BABIES
Histon
Cottenham
(B1049)
Arbury
Kings Hedges
Ring road
Park Street
Grafton
Diverted
traffic

Histon Road Voices

Inspired by members of the Mayfield Seniors Group

Once we could hear the plump thud
of an apple falling in the orchard,
the heartbeat
of plimsolled feet jogging round
the allotment.
'We did our courting there. Pretended
we were going to pick mushrooms.'

Once the loudest sound was an irritated
bicycle bell, or children's laughter,
coming home from school.
We heard the hammer's cheerful thud,
the show-stopping crane,
making a house in a day
for grateful prefab people.
'They only pulled them down
when Borrowdale was built.'

But house by house and car by car
the road filled up
with roars and hums and diesel fumes
and the defiant beep of the crossing
light.
'It's a bad road for bikes. It's hard to
get around
even if our knees were still up to it.'

Now these sounds trouble us:
the screech and growl of traffic snarled
across the junction.
'It's how they behave – they don't signal!
I sometimes give them
a hard stare.'

The drama-queen ambulance, the
helicopter's searchlight clamour
'I always wonder what's occurring.'

A complacent hiss from the guided bus
as it sails past, empty.
'They built up the pavement for the bus
to stop: but it never does.
We have to wait
for the number 8 to the city centre.'

The morning rush hour's slow
interminable thrum,
and the well-fed rumble of air-
conditioned cars,
carrying council fat cats with
loud opinions
about the City Deal.

But do they hear us, waiting
at the bus stop in the rain?

Marion Leeper,
Bard of Cambridge, October 2016

Acknowledgements

This book is the result of a close collaboration between members of Histon Road Residents' Association (HRARA) and the Benson Area Residents' Association (BenRA), with two committee members from each working on the text and images. Many people have contributed, and we are very grateful to them all. They include the oral history interviewees:
Clive Bowring, Karina Cleland, Alison Cox, Anna Crutchley, Norma Davies, Janet and Terry Dunn, Kay Harris, Alison Hennegan, Rosemarie Hutchinson, Barbara Jago, Marion and David Keyworth, Jo-Anne Kocian, David Lawrence, Marion MacLeod, Liz Moon, Maureen Newman, Pat and Heather Parker, Karen Ready, Lilian Rundblad, Molly Sneddon, Gabrielle and John Sutcliffe, Patricia Twinn, Ann Whitmore and Alison Wilson. Their recordings have been the foundation stone of the project and they were a delight to work with.

Their interviewers were Sarah Boyer, Alison Cox, Anna Crutchley, Cheney Payne and Alison Wilson. We had a lot of help with the time-consuming task of transcribing the recordings from Sarah Boyer, Anna Crutchley and Jane Qualtrough.

Additional valuable material in the form of text, images and contributions to our meetings has been donated by Robin Barrett, Jackie Bartholomew, Maurice Beeton, Dorothy Bicheno, Paul Brazier, Janet Bunker, Rosemary Cullum, Henry and Malcolm Dale on behalf of their father Rodney, Mahmood Mohammed Darr, Avril Dring, Michael French, Carole Jones, Marwar Kuwaider, David Lawrence, Giles Munby, owner of the Playfair Works drawing by Jon Harris, Rob Noble, Paul Pegasiou, Mike Petty, Richard Pryor on behalf of his father Ronald, Pat Stokes, Guy Turvill and Shi Weidong. Charles Alverson's family kindly agreed to the use of quotations from his website. All of this has greatly enriched the text.

We would like to thank Carol Leonard who joined us on the 'A Community Remembers' Committee for a while, and allowed us to share meetings with the Mayfield Seniors. They became valued members of the project. We are very pleased to have Marion Leeper's permission to include a poem she based on one of their meetings.

Faruk Kara's fine documentary photography has included portraiture of Janet Bunker, Anna Crutchley, Norma Davies, Avril Dring, Antony Finn, Alison Hennegan, David and Marion Keyworth, David Lawrence and his colleagues at the Old Chesterton allotments on Histon Road, Marion MacLeod, Liz Moon, Karen Ready, Lilian Rundblad, John Sutcliffe, Ann Whitmore and Alison Wilson. He also took photographs at our meetings. His work has resulted in a valuable portfolio of the Histon Road improvement project, and an exhibition at St Augustine's Community Centre.

We are very grateful to the Trustees and staff of the Museum of Cambridge for their collaboration, and to Danny Pedlar for training in oral history interviewing and the loan of a field recorder. Our recorded material will be accessioned into their collections for posterity and we hope it will be accessed far into the future. At the Cambridgeshire Collection and Cambridgeshire Archives, staff have been immensely helpful in providing key material for our research.

For technical help we are grateful to Alastair Beresford for setting up our website, to Ros Horton at Cambridge Editorial for her prompt and painstaking editorial work, and to our skilful designer Paul Allitt.

Cambridge City Council Arbury and Castle wards awarded us grants to run the public meetings during 2019 and 2020, and the Histon Road Co-operative Store gave us a Community Fund Grant to publish the book, and for those we are immensely grateful. These grants allowed us to print and disseminate publicity across the whole neighbourhood, hold meetings and donate copies of the book to all those involved in the project and to local schools, libraries and archives.

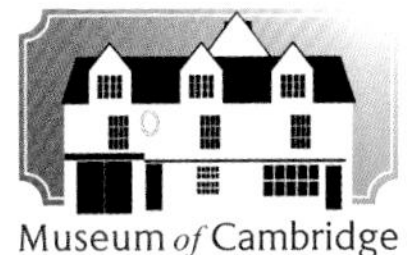

Picture credits

Faruk Kara has been our photographer for this project and nearly all the modern photographs are his copyright with the following exceptions:
Pages 75 and 128 Wayne Boucher
Page 22 Paul Brazier
Page 44 (left) Mike Petty; (right) Michael French
Pages 38 and 68–69 aerial views by Simon Martin
Permission to publish them is gratefully acknowledged.

We are also grateful to *Cambridge News* for permission to publish images on pages 4, 14, 15 (lower), 19, 23, 52, 60, 77, 90 and 96, and to *Cambridgeshire Times* for page 12.

The map on page iv is reproduced by kind permission of the Syndics of Cambridge University Library and the map on page 70 is © Crown Copyright and Landmark Information Group Limited (2021). All rights reserved (1950).

Many participants have allowed us to use their photographs and it has not always been possible to establish the copyright holders. The owners include Ann Whitmore (page 18), Carole Jones (page 20), Maurice Beeton (page 54, lower), Jackie Bartholomew (pages 102–03, 109) and her plan (page 78).

We thank Kate Challis for providing the photograph on page 65 from the *Mayfield Primary School Review*, 1972 and page 115 of Richmond Road School.

The historic photograph of French's Mill (page 25) is © Michael French.

Richard Pryor kindly gave permission for his father's drawing of Histon Road to be photographed by Faruk Kara (pages 10–11).

The photograph on page 54 (upper) is published courtesy of the Prefab Museum (Creative Commons), © John Wilson.

The photograph on page 23 is from Peter Higginbotham's *Children's Homes* website, courtesy of the owner.

The Cambridgeshire Collection at Cambridge Central Library provided the photograph on page 117.

Histon and Impington Village Society (H&IVS) have kindly provided access to images: page 111 collected by Richard Haughey of Cambridge in the 1990s and currently stored in the Philip Starling digital archive to which the H&IVS has access, and page 112, © Chivers & Co., now in the Oates Collection. Special thanks are due to Eleanor Whitehead for locating them.

Sources and further reading

Dale, Rodney, *From Ram Yard to Milton Hilton: Cambridge Consultants – the Early Years.* Haddenham: Fern House, 2010.

Forshaw, Alec, *Growing up in Cambridge: From Austerity to Prosperity. Stroud*: The History Press, 2009.

Friends of Histon Road Cemetery Newsletter. Available in the Cambridgeshire Collection.

Purkis, Sallie, *Arbury is Where we Live.* EARO, 1981.

Team Mayfield, *50 years of Mayfield Primary School.* 2012.

Websites

BBC WW2 The People's War: www.bbc.co.uk/history/ww2peopleswar/

British History Online: Histon: www.british-history.ac.uk/vch/cambs/vol9/pp90-94/

Cambridge2000: www.cambridge2000.com/cambridge2000/

Cambridge Antiquarian Society: www.camantsoc.org

Cambridge Historian: www.cambridgehistorian.co.uk

Capturing Cambridge: www.capturingcambridge.org

Charles Alverson's website: www.smart.co.uk/chasonline/

French's Mill: https://catalogue.millsarchive.org/uploads/r/null/7/c/d/7cd534f716a7ce45d5c2182eeb57919bea113de2a9c47a65398ad57581206c20/_home_artefactual_digi_objects_Rest_1116095.pdf

Histon and Impington Archaeology Group (HIAG): www.hiarchaeology.wordpress.com

Histon and Impington Village Society (HIVS): www.histonandimpingtonvillagesociety.wordpress.com

Histon Road Cemetery: www.histonroadcemetery.org

Historyworks: www.historyworks.tv

Map of the Parish of Chesterton 1840 (c. 1880): https://cudl.lib.cam.ac.uk/view/MS-MAPS-MS-PLANS-00059/1

Mike Petty's Histon Road Area Scrapbook: www.archive.org/details/CambridgeHISTONROADAreaScrapbook/

Mike Petty's Housing Chronicle: www.archive.org/details/CambridgeHOUSINGChronicle/page/n35/mode/1up?q=Histon+Road

Prefab Museum: www.prefabmuseum.uk

Rock End: www.childrenshomes.org.uk

Index

Numbers in italics indicate photographs